FEASTING

———◇———

FEASTING

A NEW TAKE ON JEWISH COOKING

AMANDA RUBEN

hardie grant books

**IN LOVING MEMORY OF MY MUM, TAMARA RUBEN
(14 JANUARY 1943 – 21 NOVEMBER 2011)**

AN INSPIRATIONAL AND REMARKABLE WOMAN WHO
STARTED ME ON THIS JOURNEY BUT LEFT IT WAY
TOO SOON. YOU WILL ALWAYS BE WITH ME.

AND TO MARK, COOPER AND MILLA

YOU LOVE ME, SUPPORT ME, MAKE ME LAUGH
AND GROUND ME EVERY DAY. YOU ARE MY WORLD – I'M
SO BLESSED AND PROUD TO BE YOUR WIFE AND MUM.
THANK YOU FOR ALWAYS LETTING ME FOLLOW MY DREAMS,
AS CRAZY AS THEY SOMETIMES MAY BE.

—◇—

CONTENTS

I DID NOT LEARN TO COOK FROM MY MUM, BUT I DID LEARN TO COOK *BECAUSE* OF MY MUM.

My mother, Tamara, was always so busy entertaining, giving cooking lessons or running an array of food businesses – from sandwich shops to food stores, catering companies, reception centres and a kosher restaurant – that she didn't really have time to teach me.

Still, I was always at her hip, and luckily, some of her amazing talent, boundless energy and love for bringing people together with food rubbed off on me.

Like myself a generation later, Mum didn't start off in the food industry. She was a medical scientist first but was never more in her element than when she was throwing lavish dinner parties for her sprawling gang of friends. Through word of mouth, entertaining at home turned into catering requests, and before long, she was running her first food business and cooking full-time for a living.

Although Tamara came from a very traditional Eastern European Jewish background – think cabbage rolls, gefilte fish and borscht – her food always pushed the boundaries to the point where she became a thoroughly modern cook well before her time.

So, I can think of no one more fitting than my beautiful, determined and hard-working mother to be the inspiration behind this collection of recipes. They are drawn from my heritage but are made for bringing together the families and friends of today. They reflect the food that I cook for my own family and friends, and the food they in turn cook for me. Based on seasonal produce, these are simple, modern recipes from the heart of my little shop and cafe, Miss Ruben, in Melbourne's Ripponlea.

Many of these dishes reflect the food of my childhood, such as the Farro and chicken cholent (page 119), which I used to eat for breakfast, or the Potato and carrot latkes (page 151), very much like the ones that my mum made to celebrate every Chanukah. But now, what we eat on a Friday night or even on Jewish holidays is so much more influenced by our lifestyles, diet and seasonal produce, and by the many parts of the globe modern Jews call home. That is no more true than in the massive influence of North African and Middle Eastern food brought to light through the fame and talent of Yotam Ottolenghi in the UK and chefs such as Michael Solomonov in the US.

As with the children of many migrant Jewish parents who came to Australia to escape post-war Europe, my parents were determined for me and my younger brother, Justin, to become doctors or lawyers. My parents could not fathom why I would choose journalism instead and my brother, the hedonistic advertising industry and a career as a copywriter.

But food was always the thread that bound us together. When Justin first went to London to further his advertising career, he bluffed his way into cooking in a gastropub to supplement his income. He remains a fabulous cook, if not a slightly messy one, to this day.

My very first journalism job was to write about food in the *Australian Jewish News*. Many years later, after a successful career writing for daily newspapers and running my own PR company, I followed in my mother's footsteps and also made my passion for food a full-time occupation.

Some of my fondest memories of Mum are of her helping out in the kitchen of my very first food business, named after my gorgeous children, Cooper and Milla. Mum, of course, was meant to be in retirement but after so many years bringing joy from the kitchen to so many people she still was too busy to stop and teach me what came so naturally to her. And, of course, she'd never heard of writing down a recipe, which is in part my inspiration for putting together this book.

This is my legacy for my own children and their children, and a tribute to all those women, like my mum and her mother before her, who filled their tables with a feast of simple, delicious food.

AMANDA RUBEN

My mum, Tamara, in a photograph taken for a book of Jewish stories and recipes she contributed to, Cooking from the Heart

My husband, Mark, and me with Cooper and Milla, my dad, Alex, my brother, Justin, and Justin's family, Giselle, Sabine and Anouk, at Cooper's bar mitzvah

STAY
HUMBLE,

DAILY DESSERT
SERVED WARM WITH CREAM OR
VANILLA BEAN ICE-CREAM $12.50

HOW TO USE THIS BOOK

It's no coincidence that a cookbook of mine is called *Feasting*. I don't know any other way to cook or eat.

As a very young girl I stayed up late in case there was an extra chocolate soufflé at my mum's dinner parties. My first memories in a commercial kitchen are of peeling snow peas for her catering business in the 1980s; she was known for her decadent coronation chicken salad, which became our biggest seller at the Cooper & Milla's food stores more than twenty years later. Our family meals were always cooked and eaten in the kitchen, with the food laid out for everyone to help themselves. At Chanukah there were doughnuts, birthday dinners always ended with those soufflés, and Shabbat meant four courses. The best thing about Friday nights at my grandparents' was the leftovers my brother and I would eat the next morning for breakfast – everything from cabbage rolls to potato kugel. On holidays, we'd spend hours at farmers' markets and roadside stalls, lugging produce back to rented houses to cook for that night's dinner. My husband, Mark, who grew up eating meat and three veg, still talks about the amount of food laid out on the table the first time he ate dinner at my parents' house.

At Miss Ruben we're known for creating picturesque, abundant grazing tables using the freshest ingredients, which is what really defines my food. And the aim of this book is to let you create a little bit of this at home, by mixing and matching the recipes to make your own feasts. The sides and starters are interchangeable; many of the mains can be adapted to serve four people or fourteen. And the signature salads often hold up as a course on their own with nothing more than some great sourdough.

Most of these recipes can be prepared with little skill. Some require a bit more effort but are well worth it, and for others you can cheat a bit and no one will be the wiser. In many of the recipes you can swap ingredients depending on what's in your fridge: asparagus for beans, feta for goat's cheese, sweet potato for pumpkin. The Roast chicken slaw (page 88) is just as good with a quality store-bought chook. If you don't want to cure your own salmon, buy some ready-made and make the gorgeous little Buckwheat blinis (page 51). But believe me, you'll never want to buy hummus or packet noodles again after you've made them yourself.

All eggs used in the recipes are 70 g (2½ oz), free range and room temperature unless otherwise specified. Milk is always whole milk unless otherwise specified, although I have tried to use a number of dairy replacements such as Home-made almond milk (page 214).

On the next few pages are some suggested menus I've designed for entertaining. They all have elements that can be started a couple of days before so you're not standing in the kitchen while your guests eat and drink.

But mostly this book is about stopping your busy lives to bring people together to eat. Enjoy.

PESACH

—◇—

PASSOVER

STARTERS

SMOKED WHITE FISH DIP // 54

DILL AND VODKA GRAVLAX // 53

CHOPPED LIVER WITH CHERRY MOSTARDA
(SWAP THE CROSTINI FOR MATZO CRACKERS) // 50

RED CABBAGE AND POPPY SEED SALAD // 74

FOLLOWED BY

GOLDEN CHICKEN SOUP (DON'T FORGET THE MATZO BALLS) // 44

MAINS

12-HOUR LAMB SHOULDER // 137

BRINED ROAST CHICKEN WITH CHIMICHURRI // 117

ROASTED BRUSSELS SPROUTS WITH SUNFLOWER SEED PURÉE // 171

MIXED LEAVES WITH SPICED NUTS AND SPIRALISED BEETROOT // 84

SWEET AND SOUR EGGPLANT CAPONATA // 177

DESSERT

FLOURLESS CHOCOLATE TORTE WITH BLOOD PLUM COMPOTE // 197

ROSH HASHANAH

◇

JEWISH NEW YEAR LUNCH

SHARING TABLE

FRIED FISH WITH AGRODOLCE // 57

SPELT PASTA WITH CAULIFLOWER AND
HAZELNUT PANGRATTATO // 107

CONFIT OCEAN TROUT WITH
PICKLED CUCUMBER AND
MINTED LABNE // 113

BURRATA WITH MIXED TOMATOES
AND BASIL OIL // 83

BRAISED ARTICHOKES WITH
WHITE WINE AND THYME // 162

DECONSTRUCTED BABA GANOUSH // 39

SAVOY CABBAGE, KOHLRABI AND
BRUSSELS SPROUT SLAW // 75

DESSERT

ROASTED PEACH, PECAN AND SPELT CRUMBLE
WITH LEMON CURD // 189

NEW YEAR HONEY CAKE // 213

YOM KIPPUR

—◇—

BREAKING THE FAST

WITH A CUP OF TEA
LEMON CHIFFON CAKE WITH
PASSIONFRUIT ICING // 207

MAINS
MISS RUBEN'S PASTRAMI // 129

POTATO AND ONION TORTILLA WITH
SMOKED PAPRIKA SALT // 59

HUMMUS WITH THREE TOPPINGS // 32

CHARGRILLED BROCCOLINI WITH
GREEN TAHINI // 175

SICILIAN BRAISED FENNEL WITH
CARROT AND ORANGE // 158

CHARGRILLED CORN, KALE AND
QUINOA WITH SRIRACHA // 73

DESSERT
ROASTED RHUBARB WITH
ORANGE AND VANILLA // 191

FRIDAY NIGHT DINNER

◇

SHABBAT

STARTERS

GOLDEN BEETROOT TAHINI // 31

CHICKPEA FALAFEL // 37

SPELT PITTAS // 167

CHOPPED SALAD WITH PICKLED CELERY,
WHIPPED FETA AND DUKKAH // 92

ASPARAGUS WITH CHALLAH CROUTONS
AND DUCK EGG // 64

MAINS

FISH STEW WITH TURMERIC AIOLI // 115

SPICED ISRAELI COUSCOUS // 153

GREENS WITH CHILLI AND GARLIC // 174

WHOLE ROASTED CAULIFLOWER
WITH TAHINI AND TOMATO SALSA // 146

DESSERT

SICILIAN APPLE CAKE // 212

GIRLS' LUNCH

◇

WITH DRINKS
BUCKWHEAT BLINIS WITH
DILL AND VODKA GRAVLAX // 53

FOLLOWED BY
GUACAMOLE WITH CHARGRILLED CORN SALSA // 149

MILLA'S SPELT AND SEED CRACKERS // 168

FRESH TUNA NIÇOISE // 91

BUFFALO MOZZARELLA WITH FIGS
AND CANDIED WALNUTS // 77

ROASTED BEETROOT CARPACCIO WITH GOAT'S CURD
AND BLOOD ORANGE DRESSING // 94

DESSERT
CHOCOLATE SWIRL PAVLOVA WITH
ROSEWATER CREAM, TURKISH DELIGHT
AND STRAWBERRIES // 204

DINNER PARTY

◇

WITH DRINKS

SUMAC AND POLENTA FRIED ARTICHOKES // 165

STARTER

POACHED VEAL WITH SAFFRON AIOLI
AND QUAIL EGGS // 138

MAINS

POMEGRANATE AND HONEY-GLAZED POUSSIN // 120

SAFFRON AND BARBERRY PILAF // 166

ROASTED DUTCH CARROTS WITH
HONEY AND CUMIN // 159

EGGPLANT TABBOULEH // 97

DESSERT

MIDDLE EASTERN FRUIT SALAD
WITH CASHEW CREAM // 201

STARTERS

TAHINI DIP

— ◇ —

Tahini – a paste made from ground, hulled sesame seeds – has been a staple in the cooking and diets of the Mediterranean and Middle East for thousands of years. It's best known as an ingredient in hummus but has come to light in recent years as a great dairy substitute in baking, dressings and savoury dishes. Similar in texture to a nut butter, tahini transforms into a creamy dip when mixed with lemon juice, salt and cold water. When using tahini in hummus or to top a meat dish, keep it thick and creamy. As a condiment for pitta or falafel, thin the dip by diluting it with a tablespoon of cold water.

SERVES 4–6

270 g (9½ oz/1 cup) tahini
1 teaspoon sea salt
1 garlic clove, finely grated
125 ml (4 fl oz/½ cup) iced water
juice of ½ lemon

Combine the tahini, salt and garlic in a mixing bowl.

Whisk in the iced water and lemon juice until thick and smooth. You can do this by hand, with a balloon whisk, or using a hand-held blender.

Serve immediately, or store in an airtight container in the refrigerator for up to 1 week.

GOLDEN BEETROOT TAHINI

— ◇ —

The golden beets add a mellow flavour but vibrant colour to tahini dip – you could do the same with red beetroot.

SERVES 4–6

14 baby golden beetroot (beets),
  leaves discarded
135 g (5 oz/½ cup) Tahini dip (see above)
2 tablespoons Dukkah (page 92), to garnish
1 candy beetroot (beet), finely sliced, to garnish
2 radishes, finely sliced, to garnish
dill sprigs, to garnish
olive oil, for drizzling
Spelt pittas (page 167), to serve

Half-fill a medium saucepan with water and bring to the boil.

Place the golden beetroot in a steamer basket and set it over the pan. Cover and steam for approximately 45 minutes, or until the beetroot is soft when pierced with a knife.

Remove the beetroot from the heat and set aside to cool before gently peeling off the skins.

Place the peeled beetroot and tahini dip in a food processor and pulse, in two-second bursts, until smooth.

Spoon into a serving bowl and garnish with dukkah, sliced beetroot and radish, dill sprigs and drizzled oil. Serve with warm spelt pittas for dipping.

HUMMUS
—◇ WITH ◇—
THREE TOPPINGS

Originating in the Mediterranean and Middle East during ancient times, hummus has become a household staple, and everyone has their own ideas of what should go into it. I'm a stickler for tradition and don't believe in anything other than chickpeas, tahini, lemon juice, garlic, salt and water. But you can elevate your hummus with any of these three toppings, each adding their own unique flavours to your humble chickpea purée.

SERVES 6–8

250 g (9 oz) dried chickpeas, soaked overnight in cold water
1 teaspoon bicarbonate of soda (baking soda)
2 teaspoons salt
½ garlic clove, roughly chopped
205 g (7 oz/¾ cup) Tahini dip (page 31)
juice of 3 lemons
200 ml (7 fl oz) iced water
sea salt and freshly cracked black pepper, to taste

Put the chickpeas in a saucepan over medium heat with the bicarbonate of soda and stir gently until it dissolves.

Cover the chickpeas with water and bring to the boil. Remove any foam that forms on the surface, reduce the heat to medium and simmer until cooked, about 30–40 minutes. Remove from the heat and drain the chickpeas.

In a food processor, combine the chickpeas, salt and garlic, and process until a thick paste forms. With the machine still running, add the tahini dip, lemon juice and iced water. Process for another 3–5 minutes, until smooth. Adjust the seasoning to taste.

Serve the hummus on its own or with a topping.

DRIED SPICED LAMB

2 tablespoons olive oil
1 small onion, finely chopped
1 garlic clove, finely grated
1 teaspoon ground cinnamon
1 teaspoon ground cumin
1 teaspoon sweet paprika
½ teaspoon ground chilli
½ teaspoon salt
200 g (7 oz) minced (ground) lamb
1 tablespoon pomegranate molasses
juice of ½ lemon
seeds of ½ pomegranate, to garnish
1 teaspoon dried spearmint, to garnish

Heat the oil in a large frying pan over medium heat and gently sweat the onion and garlic for 5 minutes. Add all the spices, fry for another 2 minutes, then add the lamb.

Continue frying the lamb to a very dry consistency, about 10 minutes. Remove form the heat, then stir through the molasses and lemon juice.

Sprinkle the lamb over the hummus and finish with the pomegranate seeds and dried spearmint.

CHICKPEA AND ZHOUG

—◇—

110 g (4 oz/½ cup) dried chickpeas, soaked overnight in cold water

Zhoug
30 g (1 oz/1 cup) coriander (cilantro) leaves and stems, finely shredded
20 g (¾ oz/1 cup) flat-leaf (Italian) parsley, finely shredded
10 g (¼ oz/½ cup) mint, finely shredded
1 long green chilli, seeds removed and finely diced
1 large French shallot, finely diced
1 teaspoon ground cumin
½ teaspoon ground cardamom
190 ml (6½ fl oz) olive oil
juice of ½ lemon
¾ teaspoon caster (superfine) sugar
½ teaspoon salt

To make the zhoug, mix all the ingredients together in a small bowl.

Place the chickpeas in a saucepan with 750 ml (25½ fl oz/3 cups) cold water and bring to the boil.

Reduce the heat to medium–high and cook for 5 minutes or until tender, removing any foam that forms on the surface.

Drain the chickpeas and mix with the zhoug until completely coated. Scatter over the hummus.

HARD-BOILED EGG, CARROT AND RED HARISSA

2 eggs
3 small carrots, cut into 3 mm (⅛ in) slices
1 teaspoon salt
1 heaped tablespoon red harissa paste
2 tablespoons olive oil
juice of ½ lemon
1 teaspoon sweet paprika, to garnish
½ teaspoon black sesame seeds, to garnish

Bring a small saucepan of water to the boil. Gently drop in the eggs and boil for 9 minutes. Drain the eggs, refresh in cold water and leave to cool before carefully peeling and cutting into quarters.

Put the carrots in a small saucepan of water. Add the salt and bring to the boil, then turn the heat down to medium and cook for 6 minutes or until very tender.

In a small bowl, combine the harissa paste with the sliced carrots, oil and lemon.

Pile the mixture on top of the hummus and sprinkle with the sweet paprika and black sesame seeds to garnish.

CHICKPEA FALAFEL

— ◇ —

This staple Israeli street food has reached gastronomic heights. Along with traditional green falafel, I've seen red, cauliflower and even mushroom falafel. Some things never change – falafel still tastes best with tahini, pickles and, for me, loads of chilli.

MAKES 30

440 g (15½ oz/2 cups) dried chickpeas, soaked overnight in cold water
1 small red onion, roughly chopped
3 large garlic cloves, roughly chopped
1 bunch coriander (cilantro) leaves and stems, roughly chopped
1 bunch mint, roughly chopped
1 bunch flat-leaf (Italian) parsley, roughly chopped
½ teaspoon chilli flakes
3 tablespoons white sesame seeds
3½ teaspoons ground coriander
2 teaspoons ground cinnamon
1½ teaspoons baking powder
2½ tablespoons salt
grapeseed oil, for deep-frying
Israeli pickles (see below), to serve
Tahini dip (page 31), to serve

Drain the chickpeas. Transfer to a large bowl with the remaining ingredients, except the grapeseed oil, and mix well.

Working in batches, blend the mixture in a food processor until it resembles coarse breadcrumbs. Test the mixture to see if it will hold together by squeezing a small amount of mixture between your fingers. If it doesn't, blend for a little longer. Shape the mixture into 35 g (1¼ oz) discs or torpedos.

Half-fill a deep-fryer or large heavy-based saucepan with grapeseed oil. Heat the oil to 180°C (350°F) or until bubbles form around the handle of a wooden spoon when dipped in the oil. Deep-fry the falafel, in batches, for 4 minutes. Transfer to a wire rack with paper towel underneath to catch the excess oil.

Serve warm with Israeli pickles and tahini.

ISRAELI PICKLES

— ◇ —

Pickles have gone from being a way of preserving the harvest to a colourful, healthy addition to many salads, sandwiches and mezze spreads.

SERVES 8–10

2 small red onions, thinly sliced in rounds
12 radishes, quartered
2 white or purple cauliflower heads, broken into florets
1 teaspoon ground turmeric

Pickling liquid
500 ml (17 fl oz/2 cups) white wine vinegar
80 g (2¾ oz/¼ cup) kosher or table salt
55 g (2 oz/¼ cup) caster (superfine) sugar

Place the vegetables in separate airtight containers. Add the turmeric to the red onions and mix until evenly coated.

To make the pickling liquid, combine 250 ml (8½ fl oz/ 1 cup) water with the vinegar, salt and sugar in a saucepan. Bring to the boil and stir for about 1 minute, or until the salt and sugar have dissolved, then remove from the heat.

Cover the vegetables in the liquid and close each container with its lid. Transfer to the refrigerator and leave to pickle for at least 1 day.

DECONSTRUCTED
◇ BABA ◇
GANOUSH

This glamorous starter is perfect for when a dip just won't cut it on your table spread.
The eggplants look amazing piled high with the spiced chickpeas and lashings of tahini.

SERVES 6–8

7 eggplants (aubergines)
3 tablespoons olive oil
1 garlic clove, finely grated
juice of 1 lemon
245 g (8½ oz/1½ cups) cooked chickpeas
1 teaspoon sweet paprika
270 g (9½ oz/1 cup) Tahini dip (page 31)
2 tablespoons chopped flat-leaf
   (Italian) parsley, to garnish (optional)

Place the eggplants directly over a stovetop flame and chargrill until completely black on the outside and soft in the middle. Remove from the heat and leave to cool.

Use a small sharp knife to make slits lengthways down the middle of 3 eggplants and gently pry them open.

Remove the skin from the remaining eggplants and put the flesh in a mixing bowl.

Drizzle 2 tablespoons of oil over the eggplant flesh. Add the garlic and lemon juice and mix well.

Place the 3 open eggplants on a serving plate and top with the eggplant flesh.

Heat a frying pan over high heat and add the remaining oil. Fry the chickpeas and paprika in the oil until crispy, about 2 minutes.

Drizzle the tahini dip over the eggplants, pile the chickpeas on top and sprinkle with the parsley, if using.

BORLOTTI BEAN AND VEGETABLE
◇ SOUP ◇
WITH SLOW-COOKED LAMB
SHOULDER AND PARSLEY OIL

The cabbage soup with top rib that I grew up eating has become cavelo nero and slow-cooked lamb shoulder in my version. Use fresh borlotti beans when they are in season.

SERVES 6-8

250 g (9 oz) fresh borlotti beans, podded
    or 100 g (3½ oz) dried borlotti beans, soaked
    in cold water overnight
4 tablespoons olive oil
1 brown onion, finely diced
1 leek, white part only, sliced
3 garlic cloves, chopped
2 celery stalks, sliced
1 fennel bulb, diced
3 carrots, diced
3 zucchini (courgettes), chopped
2 potatoes, diced
½ cauliflower, broken into small florets
1 bunch cavolo nero, stems removed, leaves sliced
sea salt, for seasoning

Slow-cooked lamb shoulder
1.2 kg (2 lb 10 oz) lamb shoulder
1 tablespoon paprika
3 tablespoons olive oil
250 ml (8½ fl oz/1 cup) chicken stock

Vegetable stock
3 medium carrots, chopped
2 large brown onions, roughly chopped
3 celery stalks, chopped
8 medium tomatoes, quartered
10 button mushrooms, sliced
1 teaspoon salt

Parsley oil
2 bunches flat-leaf (Italian) parsley
80 ml (2½ fl oz/⅓ cup) olive oil
80 ml (2½ fl oz/⅓ cup) grapeseed or sunflower oil
1 teaspoon sea salt

Preheat the oven to 170°C (340°F).

Put the lamb shoulder in a roasting tin and rub with paprika and oil. Pour in the chicken stock, cover with foil and cook in the oven for 6 hours. Remove the foil and brown by cooking for a further 15 minutes.

While the lamb is cooking, put all the stock vegetables into a stockpot with 2 litres (68 fl oz/8 cups) water and bring to the boil. Turn down the heat, then simmer for 1 hour. Add the salt then strain through a fine-meshed sieve into a container and discard the vegetables.

To make the soup, cook the borlotti beans in a saucepan of boiling water until tender, about 20 minutes. Drain, reserving 250 ml (8½ fl oz/1 cup) of the cooking liquid. Set aside half the cooked beans, and purée the other half with the reserved cooking liquid in a food processor.

Heat the oil in a stockpot over medium heat. Add the onion and leek and cook until golden, about 10 minutes. Add the garlic and cook for another minute, then add the celery, fennel and carrots and cook for a further 5 minutes, stirring regularly. Add the zucchini, potatoes, cauliflower, cavelo nero and 1½ litres (51 fl oz/6 cups) vegetable stock. Season with salt, bring to the boil and simmer for around 1 hour, until the vegetables are soft. Add the reserved borlotti beans and cook for a further 30 minutes, then add the bean purée.

To make the parsley oil, plunge the parsley into a saucepan of boiling salted water for 15 seconds, then immediately transfer to a bowl of iced water. Drain the parsley and pat dry with paper towel. Place the parsley, oils and salt in a food processor and pulse for 45 seconds. Strain the oil into a container through a fine-meshed sieve lined with muslin (cheesecloth).

To serve, pull the lamb apart, scattering generously over each bowl of soup, and drizzle with the parsley oil.

THREE MUSHROOM SOUP
◇ WITH ◇
TRUFFLE OIL

My mum gave a lot of cooking lessons and demonstrations over the years and this dish was always on the list of things she taught. It's a heartwarming, healthy winter soup made extra luxurious with the truffle oil. If truffles aren't your thing, drizzle with some tahini instead.

SERVES 6-8

100 g (3½ oz) porcini mushrooms
90 ml (3 fl oz) olive oil
1 brown onion, finely diced
1 garlic clove, finely diced
2 celery stalks, finely diced
1 leek, finely diced
500 g (1 lb 2 oz) Swiss brown mushrooms, roughly chopped
500 g (1 lb 2 oz) field mushrooms, roughly chopped
500 g (9 oz) button mushrooms, roughly chopped
5 thyme sprigs
1 teaspoon salt
¼ teaspoon freshly cracked black pepper
truffle oil, for drizzling
3 tablespoons chopped flat-leaf (Italian) parsley, to garnish

Mushroom stock
1 tablespoon olive oil
2 carrots, roughly chopped
1 onion, roughly chopped
3 celery stalks, roughly chopped
6 tomatoes, roughly chopped
20 Swiss brown mushrooms, roughly chopped
10 whole dried shiitake mushrooms
sea salt and freshly cracked black pepper, to taste

To make the mushroom stock, heat the oil in a large saucepan over medium heat. Add the chopped vegetables and shiitake mushrooms and sauté for 5 minutes, then cover with 2.5 litres (85 fl oz/10 cups) water. Bring to the boil, then reduce the heat to medium–low and simmer for 1 hour. Season with salt and pepper, then strain the stock through a fine-meshed sieve into a clean saucepan, and discard the vegetables.

Add the porcini mushrooms to 250 ml (8½ fl oz/1 cup) boiling water and set aside for 20 minutes.

Heat the olive oil in a stockpot over medium heat, then add the onion, garlic, celery and leek and cook for 15 minutes, until soft and caramelised.

Drain and roughly chop the porcini mushrooms, then add to the stockpot with the rest of the mushrooms. Cook until soft, about 10 minutes.

Add the thyme and cook for a further 5 minutes to release its flavour.

Pour enough stock into the pot to just cover the mushrooms and stir well. Cook for approximately 40 minutes, topping up the stock if necessary to keep the mushrooms covered. Stir in the salt and pepper, then take off the heat.

Allow the soup to cool slightly before pouring half into a blender. Blend until creamy, then pour it back into the remaining soup before giving it a final stir.

Serve in individual bowls, drizzle each bowl with the truffle oil and garnish with the parsley.

GOLDEN CHICKEN SOUP

◇

My mum always used chicken soup as an analogy for life and bringing up children: 'It's only going to be as good as what goes into it,' she'd say. This one is full of love and goodness. It's best made the day before serving.

MAKES 5 LITRES (170 FL OZ/21 CUPS)

6 chicken carcasses
1 kg (2 lb 3 oz) chicken wings or drummettes
1 whole chicken
1 kg (2 lb 3 oz) beef or veal topside (round steak)
6 carrots, roughly chopped
2 celery stalks, with leaves, roughly chopped
2 parsnips, roughly chopped
2 leeks, white part only, roughly chopped
1 onion, halved
1 bunch flat-leaf (Italian) parsley, roughly chopped
1 bunch dill, roughly chopped, plus extra
  to garnish
3 tablespoons salt, plus extra to taste
Matzo balls (page 47), to serve
Home-made egg noodles (page 46), to serve

Wash the chicken carcasses to remove any impurities and place in a large 8–10 litre (270–338 fl oz) stockpot. Cover with cold water, leaving a gap of 2.5 cm (1 in) at the top of the pot. Bring to the boil and remove any foam that rises to the surface.

Add the rest of the ingredients, reduce the heat to medium–low, cover, and simmer for 3 hours. Taste for seasoning, adding more salt if needed. Remove from the heat.

Use tongs to transfer all the chicken and meat to a large board. Leave it to cool for 15 minutes, then pick the chicken and meat off the bones and tear it into bite-sized pieces. Place in an airtight container.

Remove the vegetables from the pot. Set aside any that you want to serve with the soup, placing them in a separate airtight container, and discard the rest.

Strain the soup through a fine-meshed sieve into a third large airtight container. Close the lid and transfer to the refrigerator to cool overnight, along with the containers of chicken and vegetables.

When you're ready to serve, skim the fat off the surface of the soup and pour into a large stockpot. Bring to the boil over medium–high heat. Add the matzo balls and reduce the heat to medium. Add the chicken and vegetables, and simmer for 10 minutes, until the matzo balls are heated through.

Arrange the noodles in serving bowls and ladle over the hot soup and matzo balls. Top with fresh dill sprigs.

HOME-MADE EGG NOODLES

---◇---

Your kids will never let you buy packaged noodles again after they try this home-made version. Use good-quality eggs for an even tastier result.

MAKES 450 G (1 LB)

250 g (9 oz/2 cups) Tipo 00 flour, plus extra for dusting
3 large eggs, approximately 185 g (6½ oz) in total
¼ teaspoon salt, plus extra for cooking the pasta
olive oil, for drizzling

Place the flour in a mound on a clean surface and make a well in the centre. Crack the eggs into the well, add the salt and beat lightly with a fork. Gradually mix the flour into the eggs using the fork.

Bring the dough together into a soft ball using your hands. If it feels a bit dry, add 1 teaspoon water.

Knead the dough well for 10 minutes, or until it is smooth, shiny and elastic. Wrap the dough in plastic wrap and put it in the refrigerator to rest for 30 minutes.

Divide the dough into quarters, and re-wrap three quarters in the plastic wrap.

On a lightly floured surface, roll out the remaining quarter of dough into a thin, even circle about 3 mm (⅛ in) thick. Leave to dry out for 15 minutes. Repeat with the remaining pasta dough so you have 4 circles.

When dry, use a small sharp knife to cut the dough into noodles about 5 mm (¼ in) wide.

Bring a large saucepan of water to a rolling boil. Add 1 tablespoon salt, then add the noodles and cook for 4–5 minutes, until just tender. Drain immediately and drizzle with a little olive oil to stop the noodles from sticking.

Serve with Golden chicken soup (page 44).

MATZO BALLS

—◇—

These are the traditional accompaniment to chicken soup, particularly at Pesach, when many abstain from leaven. Nothing polarises Jewish cooks like matzo balls: fluffy, hard, floaters, sinkers, coarse, fine, small or large, and the list of variations goes on. This is my recipe from Miss Ruben – they are giant and fluffy.

MAKES 16

110 g (4 oz/¾ cup) fine matzo meal
90 g (3 oz/¾ cup) coarse matzo meal
2 teaspoons baking powder
1 teaspoon salt
½ teaspoon white pepper
6 large eggs, beaten
60 ml (2 fl oz/¼ cup) vegetable oil

Combine the matzo meals, baking powder, salt and the white pepper in a bowl.

In another bowl, whisk together the beaten eggs and vegetable oil, then pour into the bowl with the dry ingredients. Mix gently with a wooden spoon.

Roll the mixture into 45 g (1½ oz) balls, and set aside on a baking tray.

Fill a large stockpot with salted water, and bring to the boil.

Once the water is boiling, carefully drop in the matzo balls. Reduce the heat to a simmer and cover the pot with a lid or foil. Simmer the balls for 45–50 minutes.

Remove the stockpot from the heat and lift the balls out of the water with a slotted spoon. Transfer them to a plate and leave to cool.

Serve with Golden chicken soup (page 44).

Note: You can easily vary the flavour of these matzo balls. Try adding 2 teaspoons ground cinnamon and 2 tablespoons chopped dill, or 2 teaspoons ground turmeric and 2 tablespoons chopped flat-leaf (Italian) parsley, to the mixture before you roll the balls.

CHOPPED LIVER
— ◇ WITH ◇ —
CHERRY MOSTARDA AND CROSTINI

One of the best-known Jewish foods, chopped liver was originally made from goose liver.
Today it's been replaced by chicken liver, combined with onions, eggs and seasoning. I
like my onions soft, golden and sweet, and I still put the ingredients through a mincer.
Take a modern approach and serve chopped liver with this sweet-tart cherry mostarda,
which is also great on toasted challah or a bagel smeared with ricotta.

SERVES 8–10

8 eggs
125 ml (4 fl oz/½ cup) olive oil, plus extra
  if needed
1 kg (2 lb 3 oz) chicken livers
5 onions, thinly sliced
sea salt, to season

Cherry mostarda
1 kg (2 lb 3 oz) fresh cherries, pitted
80 g (2¾ oz/⅓ cup) caster (superfine) sugar
80 ml (2½ fl oz/⅓ cup) balsamic vinegar
60 ml (2 fl oz/¼ cup) full-bodied red wine
1½ teaspoons salt
½ teaspoon freshly cracked black pepper
¼ teaspoon ground allspice
2 tablespoons dijon mustard

Crostini
1 day-old rustic sourdough loaf, like pane di casa,
  refrigerated
2 tablespoons olive oil
½ teaspoon sea salt

Fill a saucepan with water and bring to the boil. Gently
add the eggs and boil for 9 minutes, then drain and
refresh in cold water. Peel the eggs and set aside to
cool completely.

Heat half the oil in a heavy-based frying pan over high
heat. Add the livers and fry for 6 minutes, or until they
are browned on both sides and just pink in the middle.
Transfer the livers to a plate and leave to cool.

Heat the remaining oil in the frying pan over medium
heat. Add the onions and sauté until just coloured.
Reduce the heat to low and season with salt and
pepper. Continue to cook the onions until sticky and
translucent, about 30 minutes.

Pass the peeled eggs and livers through a mincer and
transfer to a mixing bowl. If you do not have a mincer,
you can use a food processor to pulse the eggs and
livers to a coarse consistency, but be careful not to over-
blend to a paste.

Finely chop the cooked onions and add to the egg and
liver mixture. Season to taste with salt, and add a little
extra oil if the mixture is too dry. Mix well.

To make the mostarda, combine all the ingredients,
except the mustard, in a small heavy-based saucepan.
Bring to a simmer over medium heat, then reduce the
heat to low and cook until reduced to a thick purée (the
consistency of tomato sauce or ketchup). This should
take about 1 hour.

Take the saucepan off the heat, stir in the mustard and
check the seasoning.

If you prefer a smoother texture, pulse the mostarda in a
food processor.

>>

>> Preheat the to 170°C (340°F).

To make the crostini, trim all the crust off the loaf of bread until you have a rectangle approximately 4 × 8 × 20 cm (1½ × 3¼ × 8 in).

With a short 4 cm (1½ in) end facing you, cut long, thin slices, about 5 mm (¼ in) thick. You should get about 15 slices in total.

Line two baking trays with baking paper and arrange the bread slices on the tray as close to each other as possible. Drizzle the oil over the bread and sprinkle with the sea salt.

Bake for 20 minutes, then transfer the crostini to a wire rack to cool completely.

To serve, pile the chopped liver mixture on a platter and serve with crostini and a bowl of mostarda on the side.

Note: When making the crostini, you can also sprinkle the bread with poppy seeds, fennel seeds, chilli flakes, paprika, finely chopped dill or finely grated parmesan. Experiment and see what flavours you like.

Both the mostarda and the crostini will keep for up to 2 weeks in an airtight container in the refrigerator.

BUCKWHEAT BLINIS

—◇—

I've eaten a lot of canapés in my day but nothing beats perfect bite-sized blinis topped with gravlax, crème fraîche and – dare I say – caviar, or more realistically, salmon eggs. The buckwheat flour gives these blinis a slightly nutty flavour.

MAKES 30

100 g (3½ oz/¾ cup) buckwheat flour
75 g (2¾ oz/½ cup) plain (all-purpose) flour
2 teaspoons caster (superfine) sugar
1 teaspoon salt
2 teaspoons dried yeast
2 eggs, separated
250 ml (8½ fl oz/1 cup) milk
Dill and vodka gravlax (page 53), to serve
crème fraîche, to serve
caviar or salmon eggs, to serve
dill sprigs, to garnish

Mix together the flours, sugar, salt and yeast in a bowl.

In a large bowl, whisk the egg whites until stiff peaks form.

Add the egg yolks to the flour mixture and mix until combined. Gently fold in the egg whites using a metal spoon.

Set the mixture aside to prove for 1 hour, or until bubbles begin to appear on the surface.

Heat a large non-stick frying pan over medium–high heat. Drop tablespoons of the blini mixture into the pan to create 3 cm (1¼ in) blinis. Cook for 30 seconds, then flip the blinis over and cook for another 30 seconds on the other side. Transfer straight to a serving plate and leave to cool completely. Repeat until all the batter is used.

Serve the blinis topped with gravlax, crème fraîche and caviar or salmon eggs.

Pictured on page 52.

DILL AND VODKA GRAVLAX

——◇——

I've been making this gravlax since my days at Cooper & Milla's and we haven't changed the recipe. It's a house specialty at Miss Ruben, hand-sliced fresh every day on bagels – of course – and as a side to eggs, or sold by itself in take-home packets. We're also known for our gravlax served on grazing tables at events – no matter how much there is, it goes every time. It needs to be refrigerated for 48 hours.

SERVES 8–10

1 × 1.3 kg (2 lb 14 oz) side of salmon, pin-boned
(ask your fishmonger to do this for you)
800 g (1 lb 12 oz) salt
340 g (12 oz) light brown sugar
340 g (12 oz/1½ cups) caster (superfine) sugar
2 star anise
1 tablespoon ground cumin
1 tablespoon ground coriander
5 thyme sprigs
1 bunch dill, finely chopped
zest of 1 orange
zest of 1 lemon
4 ml (¼ fl oz) vodka
Buckwheat blinis (page 51), to serve
Herby quark (page 151), to serve
salmon eggs or caviar, to serve
1 egg, hard-boiled and finely grated, to garnish
Microgreens, for example lemon balm, to garnish
½ red onion, finely diced, to garnish
2 radishes, finely sliced, to garnish
Crispy capers (page 138), to garnish

Rinse the salmon under cold running water and pat dry with paper towel.

Combine the salt, sugars, star anise, ground spices, thyme, dill and orange and lemon zests in a bowl to make the curing mixture.

Spread half the curing mixture on a sheet of plastic wrap. Place the fish on top, skin side down.

Spread the rest of the curing mixture evenly over the flesh of the fish, massaging it in well.

Drizzle the vodka over the salmon and wrap it tightly in the plastic wrap. Place it skin-side down in a large baking dish.

Place a flat glass or ceramic dish on top of the salmon and weigh the dish down with a couple of plates or heavy books. Refrigerate for 48 hours.

Unwrap the salmon and rinse off all the curing mixture under cold water. Pat the fish dry with paper towel.

To serve, cut the salmon diagonally into paper-thin slices.

Pile slices of gravlax onto individual buckwheat blinis, top with the herby quark and salmon eggs or caviar, then garnish with the grated egg, microgreens, onion, radish and crispy capers.

SMOKED WHITE FISH DIP

———◇———

This American deli icon can easily be re-created at home. Smoking the fish is so simple – once you've made this, you'll never go back to the store-bought variety.

SERVES 6-8

2 tablespoons salt, plus extra for seasoning
500 g (1 lb 2 oz) Spanish mackerel
   or other oily fish
1 tarragon sprig, leaves picked and chopped
1 tablespoon finely chopped flat-leaf (Italian)
   parsley
1 tablespoon finely chopped chives
½ celery stalk, finely diced
½ teaspoon horseradish
90 g (3 oz/⅓ cup) Mayonnaise (page 88)
1 tablespoon capers in brine, drained and chopped
pinch of sweet paprika
3 shakes Tabasco or other hot sauce, plus extra
   to taste
juice of 1 lemon, plus extra to taste
sea salt, to taste
Milla's spelt and seed crackers, to serve
   (page 168)

180 g (6½ oz/2 cups) gourmet wood chips

Preheat the oven to 180°C (350°F).

Rub the salt all over the fish on both sides and put the fish in the fridge to brine. After 30 minutes, wash off the salt and pat the fish dry with paper towel.

Spread the wood chips over the bottom of a roasting tray, place a wire rack on top and rest the fish on the wire rack.

Place the tray over the stovetop flame until it smokes, then quickly cover the tray with foil, trapping the smoke inside. Remove from the heat and transfer the tray to the preheated oven.

After 20 minutes, check to see if the fish is cooked all the way through (it should be firm and white in colour). Return it to the oven for a further 5 minutes if required, then remove and set aside to cool.

To make the dip, flake the cooled fish into a mixing bowl and gently mix in the remaining ingredients.

Adjust the seasoning, adding Tabasco, lemon juice and salt accordingly.

Serve in a bowl with Milla's spelt and seed crackers on the side.

Note: You can source the gourmet wood chips at specialty food stores or delicatessens.

FRIED FISH WITH AGRODOLCE

My mum spent her childhood in Israel and always told us how my grandfather would keep carp in their bathtub! Fish has always been prominent in the Jewish diet and it is a custom to eat fish on a Friday night. I make this dish for Rosh Hashanah lunch with john dory, my favourite fish, but any firm white fish would work. Agrodolce is an Italian sweet and sour sauce that goes well with many things.

SERVES 6-8

750 g (1 lb 11 oz) john dory or other firm white fish, cut into small fillets
65 g (2¼ oz/½ cup) potato flour
100 ml (3½ fl oz) olive oil
sea salt, to taste
2 lemons, peeled and segmented, to garnish
dill sprigs, to garnish

Agrodolce
2 tablespoons pine nuts
180 ml (6 fl oz) white wine vinegar
1 long French shallot, thinly sliced into rings
3 tablespoons currants
55 g (2 oz/¼ cup) raw sugar

Preheat the oven to 180°C (350°F).

To make the agrodolce, firstly spread the pine nuts on a baking tray lined with baking paper and transfer it to the oven. Toast the pine nuts for 2–3 minutes, turning once, until golden brown. Watch them carefully because they burn easily. Remove from the oven and set aside.

Combine the vinegar and sugar in a small saucepan over medium heat. Simmer until the sugar has completely dissolved, about 12 minutes.

Put the sliced shallot in a small bowl and pour over the warm vinegar dressing. Add the currants and stir briefly to combine. Leave to sit for 5 minutes. Add the toasted pine nuts and mix well.

To prepare the fish, evenly coat the fillets in potato flour, then shake to remove any excess. Place on a baking tray lined with baking paper.

Heat the oil in a large non-stick frying pan over medium–high heat. Fry the fish fillets, in batches if necessary, for 2–3 minutes on each side, until just golden brown and crispy.

Transfer the cooked fillets to a baking tray lined with paper towel to soak up the excess oil.

To serve, arrange the fillets on a platter and spoon over the agrodolce. Season generously with salt and garnish with lemon segments and dill sprigs.

TUNA EMPANADAS

◇

Little pies are the ultimate Jewish finger food and every country's Jewish population has their signature recipe. I grew up eating potato piroshki and meat kreplach, both of Eastern European origin. Sephardic Jews were known for their bourekas, sambusak and filos. There's some great store-bought pastry around, but for a special occasion it's still well worth the effort to make your own. These tuna empanada are seriously tasty and best served hot, straight from the oven.

MAKES 12

Pastry
335 g (12 oz/2¼ cups) plain (all-purpose) flour, plus extra for dusting
1½ teaspoons salt
115 g (4 oz) cold unsalted butter, cut into 1 cm (½ in) cubes
1 large egg
80 ml (2½ fl oz/⅓ cup) iced water
1 tablespoon white vinegar
1 egg yolk, for glazing

Tuna filling
425 g (15 oz) tinned tuna in oil, drained
1 roasted red capsicum (bell pepper), peeled, seeded and diced into 1 cm (½ in) pieces
30 g (1 oz/¼ cup) pitted green olives, sliced lengthways
1 bunch flat-leaf (Italian) parsley, shredded
2 tablespoons olive oil
1 onion, finely diced
1 garlic clove, finely diced
¼ teaspoon dried oregano
¼ teaspoon ground cumin
35 g (1¼ oz/¼ cup) green sultanas (golden raisins)
3 eggs, whole
1 egg, beaten
sea salt, to taste

To make the pastry, sift the flour and salt into a large bowl and blend in the butter with your fingertips or a pastry blender until the mixture resembles coarse crumbs.

In a small bowl, whisk together the egg, iced water and vinegar, then add to the flour mixture. Stir with a fork until just incorporated.

Turn out the mixture onto a lightly floured surface and knead gently with the heel of your hand, just once or twice, to bring the dough together. Flatten it into a rectangle, wrap in plastic wrap, and chill it in the refrigerator for at least 1 hour.

To make the tuna filling, combine the drained tuna in a bowl with the capsicum, olives and parsley and mix well.

Heat the olive oil in a small saucepan over medium heat. Sauté the onion and garlic for 10–15 minutes, stirring regularly, until softened and slightly brown.

Add the onion and garlic to the tuna mixture, then mix in the oregano, cumin and green sultanas. Mix through half the beaten egg, season to taste and set aside.

Fill a saucepan with 1 litre (34 fl oz/4 cups) water and bring to the boil. Gently place the 3 whole eggs into the water and boil for 9 minutes. Drain the eggs and refresh in cold water, then peel. When cool, cut each egg into quarters.

Preheat the oven to 180°C (350°F).

Remove the dough from the refrigerator. Lightly dust a surface with flour and use a rolling pin to roll out the dough to a 3 mm (⅛ in) thickness. Use an 11 cm (4¼ in) cookie cutter to cut 12 circles out of the dough.

Place 1 tablespoon of filling in the centre of each dough circle. Moisten the edges with the remaining beaten egg and fold over to make a semi-circle. Crimp the edges with a fork to seal. Transfer the empanadas to a lined baking tray, brush the tops with egg yolk and bake for 15 minutes, or until golden brown.

POTATO AND ONION TORTILLA
— ◇ WITH ◇ —
SMOKED PAPRIKA SALT

This Spanish-style omelette is made creamy and delicious through cooking the potatoes in olive oil. It's a great addition to any Mediterranean spread.

SERVES 4

500 ml (17 fl oz/2 cups) olive oil
3 onions, sliced
1 kg (2 lb 3 oz) roasting potatoes, such as
   Dutch creams or desiree, peeled and cut into
   2 cm (¾ in) cubes
6 eggs
½ teaspoon salt

Smoked paprika salt
1½ teaspoons smoked paprika
1 teaspoon sea salt

Heat the oil in a large non-stick frying pan over medium heat. Add the onion and potatoes. Gently fry for 15 minutes, until the potatoes are soft, but not brown.

Whisk the eggs in a large bowl with the salt.

Drain the onion and potatoes through a colander, reserving the oil.

Allow the onion and potatoes to cool to room temperature before adding them to the egg mixture and stirring until combined.

Heat 2 tablespoons of the reserved cooking oil in the same frying pan over medium–high heat. Once the oil is hot, pour the mixture into the pan, allowing the egg to bubble up in the hot oil.

Use a wooden spatula to gently bring in the edges of the mixture as it cooks, to give the tortilla its classic rounded shape. Reduce the heat to low to allow the eggs to cook through, about 15 minutes.

Remove the pan from the heat and place a large dinner plate face-down on top of the tortilla. Quickly invert the pan to flip the tortilla onto the plate, then slide the tortilla back into the pan, return it to the heat, and cook the other side for a further 5 minutes.

To make the smoked paprika salt, combine the smoked paprika and salt in a small bowl.

To serve, slide the tortilla onto a plate, cut it into slices and sprinkle with the smoked paprika salt.

GRAPE, GOAT'S CHEESE
◇ AND ◇
ONION JAM PIZZETTE

If you've never tried roasted red grapes, you're in for a treat. Teamed with goat's cheese, onion jam and fresh thyme, these super-thin pizzette make a very sophisticated snack and are especially good teamed with a glass of rosé.

MAKES 3

400 g (14 oz) strong flour
2 teaspoons fast-acting or instant dried yeast
2 tablespoons olive oil, plus extra for greasing
1 teaspoon salt
240 g (8½ oz/¾ cup) onion jam
200 g (7 oz) goat's cheese
200 g (7 oz) small red grapes (if large, cut them in half)
6 thyme sprigs
extra-virgin olive oil, for drizzling
sea salt, for seasoning

In a large bowl, combine the flour and yeast with the olive oil and salt.

Add 250 ml (8½ fl oz/1 cup) lukewarm water and use a spatula to bring the mixture together to form a dough.

Tip out the dough onto a lightly oiled surface and, with lightly oiled hands, knead the dough for 5 minutes, or until it is soft and elastic.

Divide the dough into three pieces – approximately 200 g (7 oz) each – then cover with a damp tea towel (dish towel) and leave to prove in a warm place for 45 minutes, or until nearly doubled in size.

Preheat the oven to 250°C (480°F) and line two baking trays with baking paper.

Stretch each dough ball into a rectangle measuring approximately 12 × 36 cm (4¾ × 1 ft 2½ in), and transfer to the baking trays.

Spread the onion jam evenly on each rectangle of dough. Top with dollops of goat's cheese, grapes and a few sprigs of thyme on each. Drizzle with extra-virgin olive oil and season generously with salt.

Bake in the oven for 10–12 minutes, until the crusts are slightly browned on the edges.

Remove the pizzette from the oven, drizzle each with a little more extra-virgin olive oil and serve immediately.

CHICKPEA PANCAKE
—◇ WITH ◇—
MACHE, ASPARAGUS AND MANCHEGO

I was inspired to create this dish by something similar that I ate at one of my favourite Melbourne restaurants, Embla. Besan (chickpea flour) is gluten-free and is available at health food stores, and you will find manchego at gourmet cheese shops or good delicatessens. This dish is best eaten hot, straight from the oven.

MAKES 2

250 g (9 oz/2¼ cups) besan (chickpea flour)
1 teaspoon salt, plus extra for seasoning
60 ml (2 fl oz/¼ cup) olive oil
1 rosemary sprig, leaves picked and roughly chopped
100 g (3½ oz) mache (lamb's lettuce) or butter lettuce
100 g (3½ oz) asparagus, thinly sliced lengthways
60 g (2 oz) manchego cheese, to serve

Dressing
1 teaspoon white balsamic vinegar
60 ml (2 fl oz/¼ cup) olive oil
sea salt and freshly cracked black pepper, to taste

Combine the besan and salt in a mixing bowl. Gradually add 750 ml (25½ fl oz/3 cups) water, whisking constantly, until you have a thin, smooth batter. Set aside to stand for 40 minutes at room temperature.

Preheat the oven to 250°C (480°F).

Position one of the oven racks on the second rung from the top and place a heavy baking tray on top (this will help to crisp the pancake as it bakes).

Coat the bottom of a 20 cm (8 in) ovenproof frying pan or skillet with the oil, and place over medium–high heat for 3–5 minutes to warm the oil.

Remove any foam from the surface of the batter and discard, then mix the batter well.

Pour half the batter into the hot pan, then sprinkle with a pinch of rosemary and pepper and transfer to the oven, setting the pan on top of the preheated baking tray. Cook for 15 minutes, until golden brown. Transfer the pancake from the pan to a plate and cover with foil to keep warm. Repeat with the remaining batter to make a second pancake.

While the pancakes are cooking, make the dressing. Whisk together the vinegar and oil in a small bowl, season to taste, then dress the lettuce and asparagus.

Serve the pancakes warm, topped with the lettuce and asparagus. Grate the manchego cheese over the top and season with a little more salt.

ASPARAGUS
—◇ WITH ◇—
CHALLAH CROUTONS AND DUCK EGG

Transform your left-over challah – traditional Friday night bread – into croutons for this stylish salad featuring plump, juicy asparagus. Duck eggs have a bigger, richer yolk than chicken eggs so the flavour goes nicely with the mildness of the cheese. If you can't find ricotta salata, pecorino would work just as well.

SERVES 6–8

1 kg (2 lb 3 oz) green asparagus, trimmed
150 g (5½ oz) ricotta salata (salted ricotta)
  or percorino, finely grated
4 duck eggs
4–5 thick slices challah, crusts removed
sea salt, to taste

Lemon vinaigrette
4 tablespoons olive oil
juice of 1 lemon
1 tablespoon dijon mustard
1 teaspoon caster (superfine) sugar
sea salt and freshly cracked black pepper,
  to taste

Bring a saucepan of salted water to the boil and briefly blanch the asparagus for 1–2 minutes. Immediately transfer to a bowl of ice water.

To make the lemon vinaigrette, whisk all of the ingredients together in a small bowl.

Preheat the oven to 160°C (320°F).

Bring a small saucepan of water to the boil. Put the eggs in the pan and boil for 12 minutes. Drain the eggs and refresh in cold water, then peel. Allow the eggs to cool, then grate them with a coarse grater.

Chop the challah slices into 1.5 cm (½ in) cubes. Lay them on a baking tray lined with baking paper and toast in the oven for about 10 minutes, until golden brown. Watch them carefully because they will burn easily. Remove from the oven and leave to cool.

To serve, drain the asparagus, season with salt and pepper and dress with the vinaigrette.

Lay half the asparagus on a platter and top with half the grated ricotta, croutons and egg. Top with the remaining asparagus, and then the remaining ricotta, croutons and egg.

SALADS

ARTICHOKE
—◇ AND ◇—
GREEN BEAN SALAD

This trans-seasonal salad using artichokes, young green beans and edamame goes really well with fish. It's also great with some smoked almonds added, and for a dairy-free alternative, swap the feta for avocado. This is one of the only times I think it's okay to use tinned vegetables.

SERVES 8-10

500 g (1 lb 2 oz) tinned artichokes
2 tablespoons olive oil
300 g (10½ oz) edamame, podded
500 g (1 lb 2 oz) green beans, trimmed and
  blanched
sea salt and freshly cracked black pepper, to taste
1 teaspoon sumac
200 g (7 oz/1⅓ cups) roasted smoked almonds,
  roughly chopped (optional)
250 g (9 oz) marinated goat's cheese or Persian
  feta, broken into bite-sized pieces

Citrus thyme dressing
3 tablespoons lemon juice
2 teaspoons dijon mustard
2 tablespoons honey
3 thyme sprigs, leaves picked
150 ml (5 fl oz) olive oil
sea salt and freshly cracked black pepper, to taste

Cut the artichokes into quarters, squeeze out the excess liquid and pat dry with paper towel. Remove the outermost leaves and reserve.

Heat the oil in a shallow frying pan over medium heat until hot. Fry the reserved artichoke leaves for 2–3 minutes, until crispy. Transfer to paper towel to catch any excess oil and leave to cool. Fry the artichoke quarters in the hot oil for 5 minutes, until golden brown.

Add the artichoke quarters to a bowl with the edamame and green beans, and stir to combine. Season with salt and pepper to taste, then mix in the sumac, smoked almonds, if using, and feta, then toss gently.

To make the dressing, combine all the ingredients, except the oil, in a measuring jug. Blend the mixture with a hand-held blender until combined, then continue blending while slowly drizzling in the oil to emulsify. Season with salt and pepper to taste.

Transfer the salad to a serving bowl, drizzle over the dressing and sprinkle with the crispy artichoke leaves.

CHARGRILLED CORN, KALE
—◇ AND ◇—
QUINOA WITH SRIRACHA

This has been on our salad counter at Miss Ruben since day one and I don't think it will ever leave. Red and white quinoa combined with chargrilled corn, shredded kale and home-made sriracha sauce make this our customers' go-to salad for a barbecue or summer lunch. With its Mexican flavours, it's also great piled on fish tacos. Add extra sriracha if you like it fiery.

SERVES 8–10

200 g (7 oz/1 cup) red quinoa
200 g (7 oz/1 cup) white quinoa
1 teaspoon salt
4 corn cobs
200 g (7 oz) kale, stalks removed, shredded
200 g (7 oz) roasted pepitas (pumpkin seeds),
    plus 1 tablespoon to garnish
juice of 2 limes
75 ml (2½ fl oz) olive oil
sea salt, to taste
½ bunch coriander (cilantro) leaves, chopped
seeds of ½ pomegranate (optional)

Home-made sriracha sauce
250 g (9 oz) fresh red chilli
400 ml (13½ fl oz) white vinegar
400 g (14 oz/1¾ cups, firmly packed) light
    brown sugar

Rinse the red and white quinoa in a fine-meshed sieve.

Pour 1 litre (34 fl oz/4 cups) water into a saucepan and add the quinoa and salt. Bring to the boil, then reduce the heat to medium and simmer for 12–15 minutes, or until the quinoa has absorbed all the water and is tender and fluffy.

Chargrill the corn cobs on a barbecue chargrill plate or in a chargrill pan for 2–3 minutes on each side, or until the corn is starting to blacken in places. Remove from the heat, then cut the kernels from the cobs.

To make the sriracha sauce, remove the stem and seeds from the chillies, then place in a saucepan with 800 ml (27 fl oz) water, the vinegar and the sugar. Bring to the boil, then reduce the heat to low and simmer for about 1½ hours, stirring regularly.

Remove from the heat and use a food processor or a hand-held blender to blend the mixture to a smooth consistency, similar to tomato ketchup.

To assemble the salad, combine the quinoa, chargrilled corn, kale, pepitas, lime juice and oil in a large serving bowl. Spoon through 1½ tablespoons of the sriracha sauce, adding more if you like it spicy. Season to taste with salt, then sprinkle over the extra pepitas, coriander and pomegranate seeds, if using.

RED CABBAGE
◇ AND ◇
POPPY SEED SALAD

Serve this salad as part of a mezze selection or stuff it into pitta pockets with Chickpea falafel (page 37), pickles and hummus.

SERVES 8–10

½ red cabbage, finely shredded
1 bunch mint, finely shredded, plus extra baby mint leaves to garnish
½ bunch flat-leaf (Italian) parsley, finely shredded
40 g (1½ oz/¼ cup) poppy seeds

Dressing
60 ml (2 fl oz/¼ cup) chardonnay vinegar
125 ml (4 fl oz/½ cup) olive oil
1 teaspoon salt

Combine the cabbage, herbs and poppy seeds in a mixing bowl.

To make the dressing, whisk together all the ingredients in a small bowl.

Pour the dressing over the cabbage and mix until evenly coated.

Pile the salad into a serving bowl and scatter extra baby mint leaves on top to garnish.

SAVOY CABBAGE, KOHLRABI ◇ AND ◇ BRUSSELS SPROUT SLAW

I love the pretty shades of white and pale green in this light and crunchy slaw. Kohlrabi, a member of the cabbage family, is an awkward-looking vegetable, all knobbly and odd-shaped, but it makes this salad sing.

SERVES 8–10

100 g (3½ oz/1 cup) pecans
¼ savoy cabbage, shredded
1 granny smith apple, julienned
1 kohlrabi, julienned
10 brussels sprouts, cut in half and leaves pulled apart

Dressing
2 teaspoons cider vinegar
90 ml (3 fl oz) olive oil
1 teaspoon wholegrain mustard
1 teaspoon honey
¼ teaspoon salt
pinch of freshly cracked black pepper

Preheat the oven to 200°C (400°F).

To make the dressing, whisk together all the ingredients in a small bowl.

Line a baking tray with baking paper and spread the pecans on top. Toast the nuts in the oven for 15 minutes. Allow to cool slightly, then slice half the pecans and crumble the rest, breaking them up with your hands.

Combine the cabbage, apple, kohlrabi and brussels sprouts in a serving bowl. Add the dressing and toss until evenly coated. Add the sliced pecans and mix again.

Serve the salad with the crumbled pecans sprinkled over the top.

BUFFALO MOZZARELLA
◇ WITH ◇
FIG AND CANDIED WALNUTS

The ultimate date-night dish: sexy figs, creamy white buffalo mozzarella and decadent candied walnuts. It can all be prepared in advance, but dress it at the last minute.

SERVES 6-8

10 figs, halved
4 buffalo mozzarella balls, torn into pieces

Candied walnuts
500 g (1 lb 2 oz) whole walnuts
230 g (8 oz/1 cup) caster (superfine) sugar
10 g (¼ oz) butter

Vincotto dressing
60 ml (2 fl oz/¼ cup) vincotto
80 ml (2½ fl oz/⅓ cup) olive oil
1 tablespoon lemon juice
1 teaspoon salt
½ teaspoon freshly cracked black pepper

To make the candied walnuts, spread the nuts in a large non-stick frying pan and place over medium–low heat. Make sure they are not piled up on top of each other; fry in batches if necessary. Toast for 3–5 minutes, until lightly golden.

Sprinkle the caster sugar over the nuts, mix well and increase the heat to high. The sugar will start to melt and turn brown. Use a silicone spatula to move the nuts around gently to coat them evenly, about 5–7 minutes.

Add the butter and 60 ml (2 fl oz/¼ cup) water. It will bubble up, but this is normal. Just keep moving the walnuts, making sure they don't stick and burn.

Once all the liquid has absorbed, you should be left with shiny caramel-coated walnuts. Transfer to a baking tray lined with baking paper and leave to cool and harden.

To make the vincotto dressing, whisk together all the ingredients in a bowl.

Arrange the figs, mozzarella and candied nuts on a serving plate and drizzle over the vincotto dressing.

Note: Vincotto is a rich, thick grape syrup. It can be found in specialty food stores.

CARROT SALAD
◇ WITH ◇
AVOCADO, ORANGE AND MISO TAHINI

I love the combination of miso and tahini on top of these sweet roasted carrots, avocado and mixed seeds. Pretty as a picture, this salad goes well with meat or fish, and is superb as part of a grazing table.

SERVES 8–10

12 medium carrots, peeled
60 ml (2 fl oz/¼ cup) olive oil
1 teaspoon salt
2 tablespoons sunflower seeds
2 small handfuls of rocket (arugula) leaves
1½ teaspoons lemon juice
2 tablespoons poppy seeds
1 handful of red sorrel leaves
2 avocados, halved and sliced
2 oranges, peeled and segmented

Miso tahini dressing
1 tablespoon white miso
135 g (5 oz/½ cup) Tahini dip (page 31)
125 ml (4 fl oz/½ cup) orange juice
2 teaspoons maple syrup
1 teaspoon lemon juice
2 tablespoons iced water

Preheat the oven to 220°C (430°F).

Cut the carrots in half lengthways, then into diagonal spears approximately 1 cm (½ in) wide. Place in a bowl and mix with the oil and salt.

Transfer the carrots to a baking tray lined with baking paper. Bake for 15 minutes, or until crisp and tender.

To make the miso tahini dressing, whisk together all the ingredients in a small bowl.

Heat a frying pan over medium heat and toast the sunflower seeds for 5 minutes, or until golden.

When you're ready to serve, smear 2 tablespoons of the dressing on a large serving dish.

In a bowl, dress the rocket with 2 tablespoons olive oil and the lemon juice.

Layer the salad in the serving dish with the roasted carrots, toasted sunflower seeds and poppy seeds, then the dressed rocket and red sorrel, reserving some sorrel leaves to garnish.

Top with the sliced avocado, orange segments and more miso tahini dressing. Garnish with reserved red sorrel leaves.

BURRATA WITH MIXED TOMATOES
◇ AND ◇
BASIL OIL

Make sure you serve this salad at room temperature to make the most of the creaminess of the burrata and the flavour of good tomatoes, and allow yourself enough time to prepare the basil oil the night before.

SERVES 8–10

1 kg (2 lb 3 oz) mixed tomatoes, such as Doncaster, cherry, black Russian, or teardrop, some roughly chopped and some left whole
30 g (1 oz/1 cup) basil, torn
2 tablespoons olive oil
sea salt and freshly cracked black pepper, to taste
6 burrata

Basil oil
3 large handfuls of basil
2 large handfuls of English spinach
100 ml (3½ fl oz) olive oil
¼ teaspoon salt

Make the basil oil 1 day in advance. Using a blender or a vitamiser, finely blend all of the ingredients to a purée.

Place the purée in a fine-meshed sieve over a bowl and leave to strain overnight in the refrigerator. You should be left with a vibrant green oil.

Combine all the tomatoes in a large bowl. Add the basil and the olive oil, and season to taste with salt and pepper. Mix gently until well combined.

To assemble, pile the tomatoes onto a large serving platter and top with the whole burrata. Drizzle over the basil oil and adjust the seasoning if necessary.

Note: Burrata is a soft Italian cheese made of mozarrella and fresh cream. You can find it in specialty cheese shops or good delicatessens.

MIXED LEAVES
◇ WITH ◇
SPICED NUTS AND
SPIRALISED BEETROOT

The spiralised beetroot adds a splash of colour, making this not just another green salad.

SERVES 8-10

300 g (10½ oz) mixed leaves, such as butter lettuce, cos (romaine), radicchio or frisée
140 g (5 oz/1 cup) Spiced nuts and seeds (see below)
1 medium beetroot (beet), peeled and spiralised

Spiced nuts and seeds
155 g (5½ oz/1 cup) raw cashews
50 g (1¾ oz/⅓ cup) sesame seeds
40 g (1½ oz/⅓ cup) sunflower seeds
1 tablespoon olive oil
1 teaspoon sea salt
1 teaspoon honey
zest of 1 orange

Vinaigrette
2 teaspoons dijon mustard
2 tablespoons honey
185 ml (6 fl oz/¾ cup) olive oil
1 teaspoon sea salt

Preheat the oven to 175°C (345°F).

To make the spiced nuts and seeds, combine all ingredients in a bowl and mix well.

Line a baking tray with baking paper and spread the nut mixture on top. Bake for 12–15 minutes, or until the nuts and seeds are just golden. Remove from the oven and leave to cool and crisp up.

To make the vinaigrette, combine all the ingredients in a jug. Using a hand-held blender, blitz until the dressing is thick and emulsified.

To assemble the salad, pile the leaves on a serving platter and lightly dress with the vinaigrette. Top with the spiced nuts and seeds and the spiralised beetroot.

KIPFLER POTATOES
◇ WITH ◇
GREEN DRESSING AND HARISSA ALMONDS

This is a light and vibrant potato salad that teams nicely with fish, and goes particularly well with our Confit ocean trout (page 113).

SERVES 8–10

800 g (1 lb 12 oz) kipfler (fingerling) potatoes

Green dressing
155 g (5½ oz/1 cup) fresh or frozen peas
½ bunch coriander (cilantro) leaves and stems
½ bunch mint
3 anchovy fillets
2 tablespoons dijon mustard
2 teaspoons horseradish
juice of ½ lemon
125 ml (4 fl oz/½ cup) olive oil
1 teaspoon sea salt

Harissa almonds
1 heaped teaspoon red harissa paste
2 tablespoons honey
1 tablespoon olive oil
2 teaspoons sea salt
310 g (11 oz/2 cups) almonds

Preheat the oven to 180°C (350°F).

Put all of the green dressing ingredients in a blender or food processor and pulse, in two-second bursts, until combined but still coarse.

Place the potatoes in a large saucepan and cover with cold water. Bring to the boil, then reduce the heat to medium and simmer for 10–15 minutes, or until the potatoes are soft when pierced with the tip of a knife. Drain the potatoes and leave to cool.

To make the harissa almonds, combine the harissa paste, honey, olive oil and salt in a bowl and mix well. Add the almonds and mix until evenly coated.

Line a baking tray with baking paper. Spread the almonds over the tray and bake for 15 minutes, tossing halfway through.

Slice the cooled potatoes and transfer to a serving bowl. Add the dressing and toss until evenly coated.

To finish, sprinkle the salad with the harissa almonds.

STAY
HUMBLE
EAT

PUMPKIN
FARRATTATO
(GF)

QUINOA, CORN, KALE,
POMEGRANATE & PEPITA
w SRIRACHA DRESSING

ROMESCO & WHITE CAULIFLOWER
w FIGS PINENUTS
& SAFFRON TAHINI DRESSING

CHARGRILLED BROCCOLI,
BROCCOLINI w TOASTED
ALMONDS & A HINT OF
CHILLI + GARLIC

LIAN
TORCOLD

HOUSE MADE GNOCCHI
NAPOLI, BASIL
& BUFFALO MOZZARELLA

GREEN BEANS EDAMAME,
MARINATED FETA, ARTICHOKE
& LEMON THYME DRESSING

ROASTED BEETROOT, DUTCH
CARROTS, CANDIED WALNUTS,
LENTILS & POMEGRANATE MOLASSES

ROAST CHICKEN SLAW
◇ WITH ◇
GREEN GODDESS DRESSING AND ZA'ATAR CRUMBS

Za'atar – a herb family thought to have been in use in Ancient Egypt – is also the name of a popular Middle Eastern spice mix. These delicious za'atar crumbs can be made with gluten-free bread.

SERVES 6–8

500 g (1 lb 2 oz) green cabbage
2 medium carrots, peeled
½ bunch flat-leaf (Italian) parsley, finely sliced
¼ long red chilli, finely diced
120 g (4½ oz) fresh or frozen peas
2½ tablespoons sherry vinegar
3½ tablespoons olive oil
1¼ teaspoons salt
4 slices sourdough or gluten-free bread, crusts removed
3 tablespoons olive oil
½ roast chicken, skin and bones removed

Mayonnaise
3 egg yolks
juice of ½ lemon
½ teaspoon salt
1 heaped teaspoon dijon mustard
500 ml (17 fl oz/2 cups) grapeseed oil

Green goddess dressing
2 anchovy fillets
20 g (¾ oz/1 cup) mint
20 g (¾ oz/1 cup) flat-leaf (Italian) parsley
30 g (1 oz/1 cup) basil
30 g (1 oz/1 cup) English spinach
30 g (1 oz/1 cup) tarragon
juice of 1 lemon
¼ teaspoon sea salt

Za'atar
¼ cup sumac
2 tablespoons dried thyme
2 tablespoons sesame seeds
2 tablespoons dried marjoram
2 tablespoons dried oregano
1 teaspoon sea salt

Preheat the oven to 175°C (345°F).

To make the mayonnaise, place the egg yolks, lemon juice, salt and mustard in a food processor. Blend for 1 minute, with the motor running slowly, then gradually pour in half of the grapeseed oil in a thin stream. Add 3 tablespoons cold water and continue blending, then gradually pour in the rest of the grapeseed oil. Continue to blend until you have a smooth mayonnaise.

In a bowl mix 250 g (9 oz/1 cup) of the mayonnaise with all the green goddess dressing ingredients. Blend either in a food processor or using a hand-held blender until smooth. Store any left-over mayonnaise in an airtight container in the refrigerator for up to 1 week.

Finely shave the cabbage on a mandoline. Use a vegetable peeler to peel the carrots into long ribbons and combine with the cabbage in a large mixing bowl. Add the parsley, chilli and peas, and mix well.

Whisk together the sherry vinegar, oil and 1 teaspoon salt in a small bowl, then toss with the cabbage slaw until evenly coated.

Make the za'atar by combining all the ingredients in a bowl.

Pulse the bread in a clean food processor for 30 seconds to make coarse crumbs. Toss in the oil, 3 teaspoons of the za'atar and the remaining salt. Spread out on a baking tray lined with baking paper. Bake in the oven for 8–10 minutes, turning them halfway through, until golden brown.

To serve, layer the slaw with small pieces of chicken and spoonfuls of green goddess mayonnaise on a platter. Repeat the layers until all the ingredients have been used. To finish, sprinkle with the za'atar crumbs.

FRESH TUNA NIÇOISE

◇

This more sophisticated version of your average tuna salad is a great dish for entertaining. The rest of the salad can be assembled a few hours ahead, but leave the tuna and poached eggs until last to make it restaurant quality. Don't leave out the tuna mayonnaise. It really is the best part!

SERVES 8-10

250 g (9 oz) green beans, trimmed
300 g (10½ oz) kipfler (fingerling) potatoes
60 ml (2 fl oz/¼ cup) olive oil, plus extra to rub on the tuna
80 ml (2½ fl oz/⅓ cup) vinegar
4 eggs
600 g (1 lb 5 oz) yellow fin tuna fillets
sea salt and freshly cracked black pepper, for seasoning
2 tablespoons dijon mustard
12 baby cos (romaine) leaves
200 g (7 oz) vine-ripened cherry tomatoes, halved
squeeze of lemon
dill sprigs, to garnish
edible flowers, to garnish (optional)

Black olive tapenade dressing
80 g (2¾ oz/½ cup) black kalamata olives, pitted and finely diced
1 tablespoon capers in brine, drained and finely diced
20 g (¾ oz/1 cup) flat-leaf (Italian) parsley, finely shredded
¼ red chilli, seeded and finely diced
juice of ½ lemon
1½ tablespoons olive oil

Tuna mayonnaise
500 g (1 lb 2 oz/2 cups) Mayonnaise (page 88)
200 g (7 oz) tinned tuna, drained
1 tablespoon capers in brine, drained
juice of ½ lemon
4 anchovy fillets

Tuna spice mix
1 teaspoon fennel seeds, freshly ground
1 teaspoon coriander seeds, freshly ground

Fill a saucepan with 2 litres (68 fl oz/8 cups) water and bring to the boil. Blanch the green beans for 90 seconds, then drain and refresh in cold water. Drain again, then transfer to a plate lined with paper towel.

Place the potatoes in a saucepan and cover with cold water. Add a pinch of salt, then bring to the boil. Reduce the heat to medium–low and simmer for 12–15 minutes, until the potatoes are cooked and soft when pierced with a knife. Drain the potatoes and, while they're still warm, peel and cut into slices.

Heat 2 tablespoons of oil in a large non-stick frying pan over high heat. Pan-fry the sliced potatoes in batches, adding more oil as needed, until they are brown and crispy on both sides. Drain on paper towel to soak up the excess oil.

Cut the tuna fillet into three pieces and rub all over with oil, then season generously with salt and pepper. Heat 2 tablespoons of oil in a large non-stick frying pan over high heat and sear the tuna for about 20 seconds on each side. Set aside to cool.

Make the black olive tapenade dressing by combining all the ingredients in a bowl.

To make the tuna mayonnaise, combine all the ingredients in a food processor and blend until smooth.

Brush the tuna pieces with the mustard and roll in a bowl with the combined tuna spice mix. Slice into 1.5 cm (½ in) pieces.

Bring a small saucepan of water to the boil and add the vinegar. Reduce the heat to a gentle simmer, give the water a swirl and crack in the eggs, one at a time. Cook for 3 minutes, then remove with a slotted spoon and rest on paper towel.

To assemble, arrange some cos leaves on a plate and top with one-third of the sliced tuna, green beans, potatoes, tomatoes and tapenade. Repeat with two more layers, finishing with spoonfuls of tapenade, lemon juice and the dill sprigs. Top with the soft-poached eggs and edible flowers, if using. Serve with the tuna mayonnaise.

CHOPPED SALAD
◇ WITH ◇
PICKLED CELERY, WHIPPED FETA AND DUKKAH

While salads were never part of the cuisine of Eastern European Jews, they have become an integral part of our diets. Chopped cucumber and tomato salad is now so iconic in Israeli cuisine that it has been dubbed 'Israeli Salad'.

SERVES 8–10

10 ripe tomatoes, halved, seeded and chopped
1 large bunch radishes, trimmed and chopped
4–5 telegraph (long) cucumbers, halved, seeded and chopped
20 g (¾ oz/1 cup) dill, chopped
20 g (¾ oz/1 cup) flat-leaf (Italian) parsley, chopped

Dukkah
160 g (5½ oz/1 cup) sesame seeds
80 g (2¾ oz/½ cup) coriander seeds
60 g (2 oz/⅓ cup) cumin seeds
50 g (1¾ oz/⅓ cup) hazelnuts
50 g (1¾ oz/⅓ cup) pistachio nuts
1 teaspoon sea salt
½ teaspoon freshly cracked black pepper

Pickled celery
60 ml (2 fl oz/¼ cup) white wine vinegar
1 tablespoon salt
1 tablespoon caster (superfine) sugar
4 celery stalks, cut into 1 cm (½ in) cubes

Whipped feta
200 g (7 oz) feta
100 g (3½ oz) quark
1 teaspoon olive oil

Dressing
juice of ½ lemon
3 tablespoons olive oil
1 teaspoon sea salt
¼ teaspoon freshly cracked black pepper
1 teaspoon sumac

For the dukkah, preheat the oven to 150°C (300°F).

Spread the sesame seeds, coriander seeds, cumin seeds and hazelnuts on separate baking trays and bake for 15–20 minutes, or until lightly golden. Watch carefully because they will burn easily. Remove from the oven and leave to cool. Once the hazelnuts are cool, tip them into a clean tea towel (dish towel), fold the tea towel over them and rub gently to remove the skins.

In a blender or mortar and pestle, roughly grind the toasted coriander and cumin seeds until cracked but not powdered.

Roughly chop the pistachios and toasted hazelnuts to achieve a chunky texture. Combine all the dukkah ingredients together and mix well. Extra dukkah can be stored in an airtight container for up to three months.

For the pickled celery, whisk together the vinegar, salt, sugar and 60 ml (2 fl oz/¼ cup) water in a bowl. Add the celery and leave for 1 hour.

For the whipped feta, mix together the feta, quark and oil in a bowl, then pass through a fine-meshed sieve to make a smooth purée. Place the purée in a piping (icing) bag. Refrigerate until ready to serve.

To make the dressing, whisk together all the dressing ingredients in a small bowl.

Combine all salad ingredients in a mixing bowl and toss well. Drain the celery from its pickling liquid and add it to the salad with the dressing, mixing to coat evenly.

Pile the salad into a serving bowl and pipe dollops of the whipped feta randomly on to. Sprinkle with 2–3 tablespoons of dukkah to finish.

Pictured on page 103.

RAW GREENS AND GRAINS

———◇———

This salad is gluten-free and dairy-free and full of goodness, but it also looks and tastes great. For best results you really do need to cook all the grains separately, but if you make extra it will keep for a few days in the fridge. The toasted buckwheat adds a lovely crunch.

SERVES 8–10

200 g (7 oz/1 cup) buckwheat
200 g (7 oz/1 cup) red rice
95 g (3 oz/½ cup) wild rice, soaked overnight in cold water
sea salt, to taste
3 tablespoons sunflower oil
1 broccoli head, sliced on a mandoline
100 g (3½ oz) green beans, trimmed and finely sliced
100 g (3½ oz) cavolo nero leaves, shredded
½ bunch flat-leaf (Italian) parsley, finely chopped
½ bunch mint, finely chopped

Dressing
80 ml (2½ fl oz/⅓ cup) extra-virgin olive oil
2 tablespoons apple cider vinegar
1 tablespoon apple juice concentrate
1 tablespoon dijon mustard
1 teaspoon sea salt
juice of ½ lemon

Bring a saucepan of water to the boil and cook the buckwheat for 9 minutes, or until tender. Drain and set aside.

Bring a saucepan of fresh water to the boil and cook the red rice for 18 minutes, then drain and transfer to a separate bowl.

Finally, boil the wild rice in fresh water for 30 minutes, then drain and transfer to another bowl. Set the grains aside to cool.

Reserve approximately 100 g (3½ oz) of the cooked buckwheat, then mix the remaining buckwheat with the rices in a large bowl. Season to taste with salt.

To make the dressing, whisk together all the ingredients in a small bowl.

Heat the oil in a non-stick frying pan until hot and add the reserved buckwheat. Fry the grains until they are crispy and begin to pop, about 1–2 minutes.

To finish the salad, combine the grain mixture with the vegetables in a large serving bowl. Drizzle over the dressing and toss until evenly coated. Add the herbs and mix gently to combine. Garnish with the crispy buckwheat.

Pictured on page 139.

ROASTED BEETROOT CARPACCIO
◇ WITH ◇
GOAT'S CURD AND BLOOD ORANGE DRESSING

Swapping the thin slices of meat or fish for beetroot turns this classic Italian starter into a stunning salad.

SERVES 6-8

8 beetroot (beets)
3 tablespoons olive oil
1 teaspoon light brown sugar
100 g (3½ oz) watercress or snow pea shoots
3 blood oranges, peeled and segmented
200 g (7 oz) goat's curd, quenelled

Blood orange dressing
4 tablespoons olive oil
juice of ½ blood orange
1 tablespoon balsamic vinegar
sea salt and freshly cracked black pepper, to taste

Preheat the oven to 200°C (400°F).

Put the beetroot in a large saucepan and cover with cold water. Bring to the boil, then reduce the heat to medium and simmer for 15 minutes, until the beetroot are just tender. Drain and refresh in cold water, then drain again and leave to cool.

When the beetroot are cool enough to handle, peel off the skin and slice into thin discs.

To make the blood orange dressing, whisk together all the ingredients in a bowl.

Line a baking tray with baking paper and arrange the beetroot slices on top. Drizzle with the oil and sprinkle with the sugar, then place in the oven.

Bake for 20 minutes, until caramelised, turning the beetroot slices over halfway through. Remove them from the oven and tip any beetroot juices that remain after roasting into a small bowl. Set both aside to cool.

While the beetroot is cooking, combine the watercress and orange segments in a bowl. Dress with the blood orange dressing.

To serve, arrange the beetroot slices on a platter and spoon over the reserved beetroot cooking juices. Pile the salad on top and finish with quenelles of goat's curd. Season with a little more salt and pepper if necessary.

EGGPLANT TABBOULEH

◇

This salad screams of summer. For the best results it needs sweet, ripe tomatoes and young, firm eggplants. Make sure you roast the eggplant slices until they are golden and tender. I like to tear them up by hand and gently mix them through the burghul.

SERVES 8-10

175 g (6 oz/1 cup) fine burghul (bulgur wheat)
10 medium ripe red tomatoes, about 1 kg
  (2 lb 3 oz)
4 large eggplants (aubergines)
60 ml (2 fl oz /¼ cup) olive oil
8 spring onions (scallions), finely sliced
1 large bunch mint, finely shredded
1 large bunch flat-leaf (Italian) parsley,
  finely shredded
½ teaspoon sumac, to finish

Dressing
2 tablespoons pomegranate molasses
juice of 1 lemon
3 tablespoons olive oil
1 teaspoon sea salt

Preheat the oven to 180°C (350°F).

Place the burghul in a fine-meshed sieve and rinse thoroughly for 1–2 minutes. Rest the sieve over a bowl and leave to dry for 15 minutes.

Quarter, seed and cut the tomatoes into small cubes.

Slice eggplants lengthwise at approximately 1 cm (½ in) thickness, coat in olive oil and place on a baking tray. Bake in the oven for 15 minutes or until golden, then set aside to cool.

Combine the spring onions and herbs in a large bowl.

Slice or tear the eggplant lengthways at approximately 1 cm (½ in) thickness again to create stips. Add to the mixing bowl.

Add the burghul and tomatoes and mix well.

To make the dressing, whisk together all the ingredients in a bowl. Pour over the tabbouleh and toss gently until evenly coated. Sprinkle with sumac to finish.

MAINS

PUMPKIN AND RICOTTA KUGEL
◇ WITH ◇
HOME-MADE PASTA

Kugel is a Yiddish noun meaning baked pudding or casserole; mine gets a modern makeover with home-made pasta bound by a light ricotta custard. It's a beautiful celebratory dish. If making pasta isn't your thing, ensure what you buy is good quality.

SERVES 8–10

2.5 kg (5½ lb) butternut pumpkin, cut into 1–2 cm (½–¾ in) cubes
3 tablespoons olive oil, plus extra for drizzling
sea salt and freshly cracked black pepper, for seasoning

Pasta
2 eggs
200 g (8 oz) Tipo 00 flour or plain (all-purpose) flour
semolina, for dusting

Caramelised onions
4 tablespoons olive oil
2 onions, thinly sliced
sea salt, for seasoning
1 tablespoon light brown sugar

Ricotta custard
400 g (14 oz) full-cream ricotta cheese
5 eggs
250 ml (8½ fl oz/1 cup) milk
200 g (7 oz) pecorino, grated
pinch of grated nutmeg
sea salt and freshly cracked black pepper, for seasoning

Preheat the oven to 175°C (345°F).

Spread the pumpkin cubes on a lined baking tray, drizzle with the oil and season with salt and pepper. Mix until evenly coated and bake for 15–20 minutes, until the pumpkin is tender and caramelised. Remove from the oven and set aside 310 g (11 oz/2 cups) of the pumpkin. Mash the remaining pumpkin roughly with a fork. Set aside to cool. Leave the oven on.

To make the pasta dough, combine the eggs and flour in the bowl of a stand mixer fitted with the dough hook attachment. Mix until just combined. Wrap the dough in plastic wrap and rest in the refrigerator for 30 minutes.

Lightly dust a surface with semolina and roll out the pasta dough to a 2 mm (⅛ in) thickness. Cut the dough into 5 cm (2 in) strips, then cut into triangles.

Bring a large saucepan of salted water to the boil. Cook the pasta, in small batches, for 1–2 minutes. Transfer to a bowl as you go, and drizzle in a little olive oil to stop the pasta sticking together.

To make the caramelised onion, heat the oil in a frying pan over low heat. Add the onions and a good pinch of salt and cook very slowly for at least 20 minutes, until soft and golden. Add the sugar and cook for a further 5 minutes, until sticky and caramelised.

Combine all the custard ingredients in a bowl. Add the cooked pasta and mashed pumpkin, and mix well.

Line a 25 cm (10 in) springform cake tin with baking paper. Pour in half the pasta mixture and dot with half the caramelised onion and roughly a third of the cubed pumpkin. Repeat with the remaining pasta, onion and another third of the pumpkin, reserving the last third.

Cover with foil and bake for 30 minutes, then remove the cover and bake for a further 15 minutes or until firm. Transfer to a platter, garnish with the remaining pumpkin cubes and slice into wedges to serve.

VEGETARIAN MOUSSAKA
◇ WITH ◇
KATAIFI PASTRY

Kataifi, a kind of shredded filo pastry, plays a traditional role in Greek and Levantine treats. This moussaka is a great dish for easy entertaining: it can be made the day before, refrigerated and then topped with the pastry just before cooking.

SERVES 8–10

5 large potatoes, cut into ½ cm (¼ in) slices
sea salt and freshly cracked black pepper,
    for seasoning
5 oregano sprigs, leaves picked
4 large eggplants (aubergines), cut into 1 cm
    (½ in) slices
400 g (14 oz) feta
6 large zucchinis (courgettes), cut into ½ cm (¼ in)
    slices
250 g (8½ oz) kataifi pastry
rocket (arugula), to serve

Bechamel sauce
100 g (3½ oz) butter
100 g (3½ oz/⅔ cup) plain (all-purpose) flour
1 litre (34 fl oz/4 cups) full-cream (whole) milk
sea salt, to taste

Tomato sauce
4 tablespoons olive oil
2 large onions, finely diced
3 garlic cloves, finely chopped
2 teaspoons finely chopped ginger
2 teaspoons ground cumin
1 teaspoon ground cinnamon
¼ teaspoon ground cloves
2 tablespoons apple-cider vinegar
3 × 400 g (1 lb) tins chopped tomatoes
2 tablespoons light brown sugar

Preheat the oven to 180°C (350°F).

To make the bechamel sauce, melt the butter in a small saucepan over low heat (do not brown). Stir in the flour and cook for 1–2 minutes, until the mixture is smooth. Take off the heat.

Heat the milk in another saucepan over low heat until warm, then pour over the warm flour mixture and whisk until smooth. Place the mixture back over low heat and stir with a wooden spoon until the bechamel is thick and creamy. Season to taste with salt.

To make the tomato sauce, heat the oil in a heavy-based saucepan over medium heat. Add the onion, garlic, ginger and spices and reduce the heat to low for 5 minutes, or until the onion has just softened. Stir in the vinegar and simmer for 1 minute. Add the tomatoes and sugar and increase the heat to medium. Simmer for about 30 minutes, or until the sauce has thickened and reduced by about one third. Remove from the heat and leave to cool.

Ladle a quarter of the tomato sauce over the bottom of a large ovenproof dish. Layer over half the potatoes, placing the pieces close together to ensure that there are no gaps. Season well with salt and pepper, then scatter over half the oregano leaves. Next, layer over half the eggplant, and sprinkle over half the feta. Layer half the zucchini slices over the feta. Spread another quarter of the tomato sauce on top, then add add a layer of the bechamel sauce.

Repeat these layers with the other half of the ingredients, starting with the potatoes and ending with the remaining tomato and bechamel sauces. Finally, top the moussaka with the kataifi pastry.

Cover the moussaka with foil and transfer it to the oven to bake for 1½ hours, removing the foil for the final 30 minutes to crisp up the pastry. Serve with rocket on the side.

CHICKPEA STEW
◇ WITH ◇
KALE, TURMERIC AND TOMATOES

This hearty chickpea stew will win over even the biggest carnivores. It can be made in advance, and served with mograbiah (giant Moroccan couscous) or crusty bread for a complete meal.

SERVES 8–10

2½ teaspoons cumin seeds
1½ teaspoons coriander seeds
2½ teaspoons fennel seeds
90 ml (3 fl oz) olive oil
5 small carrots, cut into half moons
2 small brown onions, diced
6 garlic cloves, crushed
½ preserved lemon, skin only, finely diced
1 long red chilli, halved, seeded and finely sliced
2½ teaspoons smoked paprika
¾ teaspoon ground turmeric
6 fresh thyme sprigs
2 bay leaves
60 g (2 oz/¼ cup) tomato paste (concentrated purée)
375 ml (12½ fl oz/1½ cups) dry white wine
1.5 litres (51 fl oz/6 cups) vegetable stock
1½ bunches cavolo nero, stems removed and leaves cut into 5 cm (2 in) pieces
1½ teaspoons red wine vinegar
sea salt and freshly cracked black pepper, to taste

Braised chickpeas
625 g (1 lb 6 oz) dried chickpeas, soaked in cold water overnight
1 small brown onion, quartered
2 medium carrots, quartered
3 large garlic cloves, lightly smashed
2 small bay leaves
6 thyme sprigs
sea salt, to taste

Green harissa oil
140 g (5 oz) green chilli
5 bunches coriander (cilantro) leaves and stems
140 g (5 oz) caraway seeds, freshly ground
140 g (5 oz) ground coriander
1 bunch mint
250 ml (8½ fl oz/1 cup) olive oil
150 g (5½ oz) English spinach
3 teaspoons salt

To make the braised chickpeas, first drain and rinse the chickpeas in cold water. Combine with all the other ingredients in a large saucepan. Cover with cold water by 5 cm (2 in) and bring to the boil. Reduce the heat to a simmer and cook for 30 minutes, until the chickpeas are tender but still holding their shape.

Discard the bay leaves and leave the chickpeas to cool, then strain and discard the herbs, garlic and vegetables.

Heat a small frying pan over medium heat and toast the cumin, coriander and fennel seeds for about 3 minutes, until fragrant. Cool the spices and grind to a powder in a mortar and pestle or spice grinder.

Heat the oil in a large stockpot over medium heat until hot but not smoking. Add the carrots, onion and garlic, season with salt, and cook until softened and slightly browned, about 5 minutes. Stir through the preserved lemon and chilli. Add the ground spice mixture, paprika, turmeric, thyme and bay leaves. Cook, stirring frequently, until fragrant, about 3 minutes.

Add the tomato paste and cook for 5 minutes, stirring frequently so it does not burn. Add the wine and bring to the boil, cooking and scraping until reduced by half, about 2–3 minutes. Add the stock, remove the bay leaves and return to a simmer over low heat.

Allow the stew to cool a little, then pour 375 ml (12½ fl oz/1½ cups) into a blender. Add 2 cups of braised chickpeas and purée until smooth. Return the purée to the pot, throw in the kale and cook until softened. Add the rest of the chickpeas, stirring gently.

Remove from the heat and leave for 20 minutes.

To make the green harissa oil, blend all the ingredients in a food processor until a smooth paste forms.

Serve the stew drizzled with the vinegar and green harissa oil.

SPELT PASTA
—◇ WITH ◇—
CAULIFLOWER AND HAZELNUT PANGRATTATO

My head chef at Miss Ruben, Bancha Boonchuen, is of Thai origin but spent time working at one of Melbourne's most iconic Italian restaurants, Caffé e Cucina. He makes the best risotto I've ever eaten. This is his recipe for cauliflower pasta – I served it at Rosh Hashanah lunch last year and it was the most popular dish on the table.

SERVES 8–10

1 tablespoon salt
1 cauliflower head, cut into small florets
150 ml (5 fl oz) extra-virgin olive oil, plus extra for drizzling
1 garlic clove, sliced
4 anchovy fillets
½ long red chilli, finely sliced
500 g (1 lb 2 oz) spelt pasta bowties
25 g (1 oz/¼ cup) pecorino, grated, to serve

Hazelnut pangrattato crumb
35 g (1¼ oz/¼ cup) hazelnuts
55 g (2 oz/⅔ cup) fresh breadcrumbs

Pour 4 litres (135 fl oz/16 cups) water into a stockpot and add the salt. Bring to the boil and blanch the cauliflower florets for 3 minutes. Remove the cauliflower with a slotted spoon. Reserve one-third of the cauliflower and the blanching water.

Combine the reserved cauliflower with 2 tablespoons of the blanching water and blend until smooth using a hand-held blender.

Heat the oil in a large heavy-based saucepan over medium heat. Add the garlic and anchovies and fry for 1–2 minutes, until the garlic is just coloured and the anchovies have melted.

Add the chilli and remaining blanched cauliflower and cook for 5 minutes, or until the cauliflower is soft. Add the blended cauliflower and stir to mix well. Add 400 ml (13½ fl oz) of the blanching water and continue stirring until the sauce emulsifies.

To make the hazelnut pangrattato crumb, heat a frying pan over high heat and toast the hazelnuts for 2–3 minutes. Combine the hazelnuts and breadcrumbs in a blender and pulse to a coarse crumb.

Bring a saucepan of salted water to a rolling boil. Cook the pasta for 6–8 minutes, until al dente. Drain, reserving 125 ml (4 fl oz/½ cup) of the cooking water. Return the pasta to the saucepan.

Add the cauliflower sauce and reserved pasta cooking water to the pasta. Mix well to combine and heat through again over low heat.

Transfer the pasta to a serving bowl, drizzle with oil and sprinkle the hazelnut pangrattato on top. Grate over some pecorino, and serve.

WALNUT-CRUSTED WHOLE SNAPPER
◇

A classic Lebanese mixture of walnuts, onion, coriander and chilli forms the crust on this whole-baked snapper. Alternatively you could use this crust on fish fillets – just sear the fillets until almost cooked, coat with the mixture and finish off in the oven. The green harissa labne needs to be left to drain overnight.

SERVES 8–10

2 kg (4 lb 6 oz) whole snapper, cleaned and gutted (ask your fishmonger to do this)
¼ teaspoon salt
60 ml (2 fl oz/¼ cup) olive oil
3 lemons, 2 thickly sliced, 1 cut into wedges
1 fennel bulb, thickly sliced
1 teaspoon fennel seeds
juice of 2 lemons

Walnut crust
150 g (5½ oz/1½ cups) walnut halves
3 bunches coriander (cilantro) leaves
1 garlic clove, crushed
1 jalapeño chilli, seeded
1 red onion, finely chopped
60 ml (2 fl oz/¼ cup) olive oil
1 teaspoon salt
1 teaspoon ground fennel
1 teaspoon ground coriander
½ ground cardamom

Green harissa labne
500 g (1 lb 2 oz/2 cups) sheep's milk yoghurt
1 tablespoon extra-virgin olive oil
1 tablespoon Green harissa oil (page 106)
1 teaspoon sea salt

Celeriac, parsley and dill salad
1 celeriac, peeled and julienned
40 g (½ oz/2 cups) flat-leaf (Italian) parsley, roughly chopped
60 g (2 oz/1 cup) dill
seeds of 2 pomegranates (optional)
zest and juice of 2 limes
3 teaspoons honey
120 ml (4 fl oz) olive oil
sea salt, to taste

To make the green harissa labne, combine all the ingredients in a fine-meshed sieve lined with muslin (cheesecloth). Set the sieve over a bowl or container, tie the muslin over the yoghurt and leave to drain overnight in the refrigerator.

Preheat the oven to 200°C (400°F).

Place the snapper on a large baking tray lined with baking paper. Rub the fish all over with the salt and 2 tablespoons oil.

Open the cavity and fill with the sliced lemons, fennel slices and fennel seeds. Transfer to the oven and bake for 30 minutes.

While the fish is cooking, prepare the walnut crust. Put the walnut halves, coriander, garlic, jalapeño and onion in a food processor and pulse, in two-second bursts, until the mixture resembles coarse crumbs.

Heat the oil in a heavy-based frying pan over medium heat. Add the walnut crumbs, salt and ground spices, and sauté for approximately 10 minutes.

Remove the snapper from the oven. Cover the fish with the walnut crumbs, leaving the head and tail exposed. Pour over the lemon juice.

Reduce the oven temperature to 175°C (345°F) and return the fish to the oven. Bake for another 15 minutes, or until the crust is golden brown.

To make the celeriac, parsley and dill salad, combine the celeriac, parsley, dill and pomegranate seeds, if using, in a mixing bowl. Season with salt to taste.

Whisk together the lime zest and juice, honey and oil in a small bowl, then season generously with salt and pepper. Drizzle the dressing over the salad and toss until evenly coated.

Serve the fish whole with the celeriac, parsley and dill salad and green harissa labne on the side.

CONFIT OCEAN TROUT
— ◇ WITH ◇ —
PICKLED CUCUMBER AND MINTED LABNE

This is the ultimate buffet table dish – it looks stunning, tastes sensational, and can be prepared ahead of time and assembled at the last minute. To confit the fish means to cook it in warm oil, so it remains soft and flakes away, making it easy for people to help themselves. The lightly pickled cucumbers, radish and dill are a refreshing balance to the richness of the fish. If you can't get ocean trout this is just as nice with salmon.

SERVES 6-8

315 g (11 oz/1 cup) rock salt
1 kg (2 lb 3 oz) skinless ocean trout
1 lemon, sliced
1 fennel bulb, sliced
1.5 litres (51 fl oz/6 cups) olive oil

Salad
1 fennel bulb, sliced on a mandoline
6 radishes, sliced on a mandoline
juice of ½ lemon
60 g (2 oz/1 cup) dill
2 oranges, peeled and segmented
2 pink grapefruits, peeled and segmented

Pickled cucumbers
2 tablespoons salt
2 tablespoons caster (superfine) sugar
250 ml (8½ fl oz/1 cup) white vinegar
3 Lebanese (short) cucumbers, sliced on a
  mandoline

Minted labne
80 g (2¾ oz/4 cups) mint
250 g (9 oz/1 cup) Labne (page 193)
1 teaspoon salt

Vinaigrette
60 ml (2 fl oz/¼ cup) olive oil
60 ml (2 fl oz/¼ cup) chardonnay vinegar
  or white wine vinegar
1 teaspoon fennel seeds, freshly ground
sea salt and freshly cracked black pepper, to taste

Prepare a brining solution by combining the salt with 1 litre (34 fl oz/4 cups) water in a saucepan. Bring to the boil to dissolve the salt, then set aside to cool completely. Immerse the trout in the cold brine for 12 minutes.

To make the confit, place the fennel and lemon slices in a large roasting tray big enough to hold the fish. Cover with the oil and place over very low heat. When the oil reaches 50°C (120°F) when tested with a sugar thermometer, immerse the fish in the oil, remove from the heat and leave for 10–12 minutes to confit.

Prepare the salad by placing the sliced fennel and radish in a bowl and cover with water and the lemon juice.

To make the pickled cucumbers, set a saucepan over low heat and add the salt, sugar and vinegar, stirring until the sugar has dissolved. Place the cucumber slices in a bowl and pour over the warm pickling liquid. Allow to stand for 15 minutes, then drain.

To prepare the minted labne, combine the mint and 60 ml (2 fl oz/¼ cup) water in a high-speed blender and blend until smooth. Put the labne in a bowl and mix in the mint paste and salt until combined.

To make the vinaigrette, whisk together all the ingredients in a small bowl and season to taste..

When you're ready to serve, drain the fennel and radish. Build the salad by layering up the citrus segments, fennel, radish and dill, then drizzle over the vinaigrette.

Remove the fish from the oil and drain on paper towel before placing on a serving platter. Top with the salad and serve with the minted labne and pickled cucumbers.

FISH STEW
—◇ WITH ◇—
TURMERIC AIOLI

This is a version of chraime, the traditional Moroccan fish stew typically served at the Shabbat table. The fish is cooked in the spicy red sauce, giving it lots of flavour and a bit of a kick. I like to use cutlets because they don't break down, meaning the dish can be cooked in advance and served at room temperature.

SERVES 6–8

100 ml (3½ fl oz) olive oil
10 garlic cloves, crushed
1 long green chilli, halved, seeded and
 finely chopped
2 teaspoons ground turmeric
2 teaspoons sweet paprika
2 teaspoons fennel seeds
3 teaspoons ground cumin
¼ teaspoon cayenne pepper
1 teaspoon ground cinnamon
4 tablespoons tomato paste (concentrated purée)
juice of ½ lemon
4 teaspoons caster (superfine) sugar
sea salt and freshly cracked black pepper, for
 seasoning
8 × 200 g (7 oz) cutlets of snapper, barramundi or
 other white fish of your choice
1 bunch coriander (cilantro) leaves, to garnish
Spiced Israeli couscous, to serve (page 153)

Turmeric aioli
1 small garlic bulb
1 egg yolk, at room temperature
5 cm (2 in) piece fresh turmeric, peeled and
 finely grated
150 ml (5 fl oz) extra-virgin olive oil, plus extra
 for drizzling
juice of 1 lemon
½ teaspoon sea salt
½ teaspoon ground white pepper

Preheat the oven to 180°C (350°F).

Heat the oil in a large heavy-based saucepan over high heat until hot, but not smoking. Add the garlic, chilli and spices, stirring quickly for 30 seconds.

Remove from the heat. Pour in 300 ml (10 fl oz) water and the tomato paste, and stir to combine.

Return the saucepan to the stove over medium heat and bring to a simmer. Add the lemon juice and sugar, and season with salt and pepper. Leave on a low heat.

To make the turmeric aioli, trim about 5 mm (¼ in) off the top of the garlic bulb and place on a tray lined with baking paper. Drizzle with a little olive oil, then roast in the oven for 15–20 minutes, until soft. Leave to cool, then squeeze the garlic from the skins.

Combine the egg yolk, roasted garlic and turmeric in a food processor and blend for 30 seconds. With the motor still running, gradually pour in the oil in a thin, steady stream. Once all the oil has been incorporated, add the lemon juice, salt and pepper.

Just before you are ready to eat, carefully place the fish cutlets into the saucepan, mix gently, and cover with a lid. Simmer over low heat for 10–12 minutes, until the fish is just cooked.

Garnish the stew with coriander leaves and serve with spiced Israeli couscous and turmeric aioli.

Note: Any left-over turmeric aioli can be stored in an airtight container in the refrigerator for up to 1 week.

BRINED ROAST CHICKEN
— ◇ WITH ◇ —
CHIMICHURRI

After being surrounded by food all week, when Friday night comes I crave the simplicity of a well-roasted chicken. It's also one of the only meals my whole family will happily eat. Make sure you start the recipe a day ahead to brine the chicken – brining adds flavour and keeps the meat tender and juicy. As kosher chickens have already been soaked in salty water as part of the kashrut process, I wouldn't recommend brining them for fear they may become too salty. Chimichurri is an Argentinian condiment designed to be eaten with grilled meat, but is also great on roast chicken and fish.

SERVES 4–6

1 × 1.5 kg (3 lb 5 oz) whole chicken
100 ml (3½ fl oz) extra-virgin olive oil
2 teaspoons sweet paprika
pinch of salt
½ lemon
1 garlic bulb, cut in half
½ bunch flat-leaf (Italian) parsley
5 thyme sprigs
Creamed corn (no cream) (page 170), to serve
Greens with chilli and garlic (page 174), to serve

Brining solution
1 rosemary sprig
5 thyme sprigs
2 bay leaves
1 teaspoon fennel seeds
2 teaspoons whole black peppercorns
1 long red chilli, split lengthways
150 g (5½ oz) rock salt

Chimichurri
1 large French shallot, about 65 g (2¼ oz),
    finely diced
1 green chilli, finely diced
20 g (¾ oz/⅔ cup) coriander (cilantro) leaves,
    finely shredded
3 tablespoons finely shredded oregano
10 g (¼ oz/½ cup) mint
3 tablespoons red wine vinegar
90 ml (3 fl oz) extra-virgin olive oil
¼ teaspoon salt

To make the brining solution, combine all the ingredients with 2 litres (68 fl oz/8 cups) water in a stockpot and bring to the boil. Simmer until the salt has dissolved.

Remove from the heat and leave to cool completely. Add the chicken to the brine, cover and refrigerate overnight.

Preheat the oven to 220°C (430°F).

To cook the chicken, remove it from the brine and pat dry with paper towel. Rub it all over with the oil, sweet paprika and salt, and leave to rest for 30 minutes at room temperature before roasting.

Stuff the chicken cavity with the lemon, parsley, thyme and half the garlic bulb.

Place the stuffed chicken on a wire rack in a roasting tray and put in the oven for 50 minutes. Turn the chicken over and continue roasting for 15 minutes.

To make the chimichurri, combine all the ingredients in a food processor or blender and pulse to a coarse texture. Transfer to a small serving bowl.

Remove the chicken from the oven and place on a platter. Spoon over the chimichurri, and serve with the creamed corn and greens on the side.

ROAST CHICKEN BREAST
— ◇ WITH ◇ —
LEMON JAM AND CRUSHED JERUSALEM ARTICHOKES

Despite its name, the Jerusalem artichoke is not from Jerusalem – neither is it a type of artichoke. It makes a delicious alternative mash to serve with this healthy chicken breast.

SERVES 6-8

6 × 200 g (7 oz) chicken breasts, skin on
1 teaspoon salt
1 tablespoon cinnamon
1 tablespoon caster (superfine) sugar
4–6 tablespoons olive oil
freshly ground black pepper, for seasoning

Lemon jam
4 lemons, halved and pips removed
250 g (9 oz/1 cup) caster (superfine) sugar
2 sage sprigs
1 cinnamon stick

Crushed Jerusalem artichokes
1 kg (2 lb 3 oz) Jerusalem artichokes (sunchokes), peeled
2 tablespoons olive oil
sea salt and freshly cracked black pepper, to taste

Salsa verde
20 g (¾ oz/1 cup) flat-leaf (Italian) parsley
60 g (2 oz/1 cup) dill
20 g (¾ oz/1 cup) mint
1 tablespoon dijon mustard
1 teaspoon anchovies
1 teaspoon capers in brine, drained
juice of ½ lemon
3 tablespoons olive oil
½ teaspoon salt

Preheat the oven to 180°C (350°F).

To prepare the lemon jam, gently squeeze the lemons until you have 2 tablespoons of juice. Set aside.

Slice the juiced lemons thinly and place in a saucepan with 250 ml (8½ fl oz/1 cup) water. Bring to the boil for 5 minutes. Drain, add 250 ml (8½ fl oz/1 cup) fresh water and repeat the process. Drain again. Add 500 ml (17 fl oz/2 cups) water, the reserved lemon juice, sugar, sage and cinnamon stick to the saucepan. Return to the boil, then reduce the heat to low and simmer gently for 40 minutes to create a glossy jam.

Sprinkle the chicken skin with the salt, cinnamon and sugar, and season with pepper.

Heat the oil in a non-stick frying pan over medium–low heat. Pan-fry the chicken breasts, skin-side down, for about 10 minutes, or until golden and crispy.

Transfer the chicken to a baking tray lined with baking paper and cook in the oven, skin-side up, for 15 minutes.

Place the artichokes in a saucepan and cover with cold salted water. Bring to the boil over medium–high heat and cook for 10 minutes, until tender. Drain, transfer to a bowl and crush gently with a potato masher. Season well with salt and pepper. Heat the oil in a frying pan over medium heat. Add the crushed artichokes and sauté until crispy on the edges, about 10 minutes.

To make the salsa verde, combine all the ingredients, except the oil and salt, in a food processor. Pulse for 3 minutes, until blended to a rough consistency. Transfer to a bowl and gently stir in the oil and salt.

Thickly slice each cooked chicken breast and transfer to a platter. Smother with the lemon jam, top with the salsa verde and serve the crushed artichokes on the side.

FARRO
—◇ AND ◇—
CHICKEN CHOLENT

My mum was famous for her cholent; I'd wake to the smell through our house on a Saturday morning and eat it straight from the pot for breakfast. Every time I type 'cholent' into my computer it corrects to 'cholesterol', which is very fitting! But this recipe won't clog your arteries. By using chicken, it's less fatty and much lighter on your stomach than the more traditional beef top rib.

While Jewish cooking has always adapted to reflect the global cultures of Jewish people, cholent is a uniquely Jewish food – although, of course, it still has innumerable variations. The dish was designed to be prepared before the Shabbat began on Friday evening and left to cook overnight.

SERVES 8-10

80 ml (2½ fl oz/⅓ cup) olive oil
2 large onions, roughly chopped
4 veal or beef marrow bones
8 chicken thighs on the bone, skin removed
500 g (1 lb 2 oz) oxtail
200 g (7 oz/⅔ cups) lima beans, soaked overnight in cold water and drained
300 g (10½ oz/1½ cups) cannellini beans, soaked overnight in cold water and drained
330 g (11½ oz/1½ cups) farro, soaked overnight in cold water and drained
6 roasting potatoes, such as Dutch creams or desiree, quartered
6 garlic cloves
2 tablespoons sweet paprika
1.5 litres (51 fl oz/6 cups) chicken stock or water
sea salt, for seasoning

Heat the oil in a large ovenproof pot over medium heat. Fry the onion until golden brown, about 10 minutes.

Add the bones to the pot and layer all the other ingredients, except the stock, on top, sprinkling with paprika and salt as you go.

Pour in enough stock to cover the ingredients, and bring to the boil. Remove from the heat.

Cover the mixture with baking paper and a tight-fitting lid.

Preheat the oven to 100°C (210°F).

Transfer the pot to the oven and leave to cook overnight.

In the morning, remove the pot from the oven. Mix well and loosen with a little more stock if the mixture has become too dry. Check and adjust the seasoning if necessary.

Leave in the oven until ready to serve.

POMEGRANATE
—◇ AND ◇—
HONEY-GLAZED POUSSIN

My mum, a medical technologist by day, would come home from work and throw amazing dinner parties for her friends, making everything from scratch in just a few hours. The meal almost always finished with perfect chocolate soufflés – since she passed away I always order soufflé when it's on a menu in her honour, but I'm yet to have one as good as hers. Stuffed baby chickens were another one of Mum's specialties, so this poussin recipe also reminds me of her. You can buy poussin from specialty poultry butchers; if you're kosher, use baby spatchcocks instead. You need to marinate the poussin for eight hours or overnight.

SERVES 6–8

6 × 600 g (1 lb 5 oz) poussin, butterflied
sea salt, to taste
Saffron and berberry pilaf (page 166), to serve
2 tablespoons pomegranate seeds, to garnish
2 tablespoons white mulberries, to garnish
(optional)

Crispy vine leaves
8 vine leaves in brine, drained
olive oil, for brushing

Marinade
8 tablespoons honey
8 tablespoons pomegranate molasses
4 teaspoons baharat
4 teaspoons orange zest
4 teaspoons salt
300 ml (10 fl oz) extra-virgin olive oil
juice of 2 oranges

Whisk together all the marinade ingredients in a large non-reactive bowl. Add the birds and coat them in the marinade, then cover the bowl and transfer to the refrigerator to marinate for at least 8 hours, preferably overnight.

Preheat the oven to 200°C (400°F).

Place the poussins on a baking tray lined with baking paper. Pour any left-over marinade into a small jug or bowl, for basting.

Roast the poussins for 30–35 minutes, basting every 10 minutes with the marinade. Remove from the oven and leave to rest.

Reduce the oven temperature to 160°C (320°F).

To make the crispy vine leaves, soak the vine leaves in cold water for 5 minutes to remove the excess salt. Dry on paper towel, then brush both sides of each leaf with oil and transfer to a baking tray lined with baking paper. Place another baking tray on top and bake for 10–12 minutes, until dry and crispy.

To serve, divide the saffron and barberry pilaf evenly among serving plates and top with the poussin. Garnish with a little extra salt, the crispy vine leaves, pomegranate seeds and white mulberries, if using.

Note: Baharat is a Middle Eastern spice mix that can be found at specialty food stores.

ROLLED ROAST TURKEY BREAST
◇ WITH ◇
QUINOA STUFFING

Quinoa replaces traditional sourdough here to make this stuffing lighter and gluten-free.
If you eat quinoa during Pesach, this makes a great main course for your celebrations.

SERVES 6–8

2 kg (4 lb 6 oz) turkey breast, butterflied
2 medium onions, quartered
2 large celery stalks, cut as long as the carrots
2 medium carrots, quartered lengthways
500 ml (17 fl oz/2 cups) chicken stock
80 ml (2½ fl oz/⅓ cup) olive oil
sea salt and freshly cracked black pepper,
   for seasoning

Stuffing
100 g (3½ oz/½ cup) quinoa, rinsed in cold water
   and drained
1 teaspoon salt
3 tablespoons olive oil
½ brown onion, finely chopped
1 celery stalk, finely diced
1 granny smith apple, peeled and cut into 1 cm
   (½ in) cubes
90 g (3 oz/½ cup) dried apricots
20 g (¾ oz/1 cup) flat-leaf (Italian) parsley,
   shredded
1 tablespoon thyme leaves and soft stalks, finely
   chopped
1 egg
2 tablespoons chopped pistachios
50 g (1¾ oz) dried sour cherries
1 teaspoon wholegrain mustard
½ teaspoon freshly cracked black pepper
½ teaspoon caster (superfine) sugar
zest of 1 lemon

To make the stuffing, combine the quinoa with
½ teaspoon of the salt and 340 ml (11½ fl oz/1⅓ cups)
water in a small saucepan. Bring to the boil, then reduce
the heat to low, cover with a lid and cook for
12 minutes. Drain and spread on a baking tray to cool.

Heat the oil in a frying pan over medium heat and
sauté the onion and celery for 5 minutes, until soft and
slightly coloured. Add the apple and sauté for another
3–5 minutes.

Soak the apricots in 250 ml (8½ fl oz/1 cup) hot water
for about 10 minutes, until plump. Squeeze the apricots
to get rid of excess liquid, then slice thinly.

In a large bowl, combine the quinoa, sliced apricots,
sautéed onion and apple mixture with the remaining salt
and other stuffing ingredients and mix well.

Preheat the oven to 190°C (375°F).

Place the turkey, skin-side down, on a chopping board
with the pointed end facing you. Open the breast out.

Place all the stuffing left of the centre on the breast,
packing it in tightly. Fold the left side of the breast over
the stuffing and begin to roll, tucking in any loose parts,
until you have a neat log. Tie the breast at 4 cm (1½ in)
intervals with kitchen twine to secure the roll.

Put the onions, celery and carrots in a roasting tray large
enough to hold the turkey with 3 cm (1¼ in) of space
around it. Pour in the stock and put the turkey on top of
the vegetables. Rub the breast with the oil and season
generously with salt and pepper.

Roast, basting with the juices every 15 minutes, for
1½ hours, or until the juices run clear when the thickest
part of the breast is pierced with a skewer.

Remove from the oven and rest the turkey for
15 minutes, then carefully remove the kitchen twine.
Slice thickly and dress the slices with the jus.

ROAST DUCK
— ◇ WITH ◇ —
MANDARIN SAUCE

Many people are intimidated by roasting a whole duck but you shouldn't be. It takes a bit of time – and the duck needs to be left to dry out in the refrigerator overnight before cooking – but it's pretty easy. And best of all, any duck fat that's left behind will make the crispiest, tastiest potatoes you've ever eaten. I love citrus fruits, and I think mandarins are underrated. Their musky aroma adds a wonderful perfume to this sauce.

SERVES 4-6

1 × 1.5 kg (3 lb 5 oz) good-quality duck
sea salt, for seasoning

Mandarin sauce
500 ml (17 fl oz/2 cups) chicken stock
7 mandarins, 5 halved and 2 peeled and
    segmented
sea salt, to taste

Wash and trim the duck, removing any excess fat and the wing tips. Pat dry with paper towel. Place it on a baking tray, cover with paper towel and transfer to the refrigerator to dry out overnight.

Remove the duck from the refrigerator 1 hour prior to cooking.

Preheat the oven to 250°C (480°F).

Season the duck generously with sea salt, inside and out. Place the duck, breast-side down, on a wire rack in a shallow roasting tray.

Roast for 1½ hours, basting with the duck fat and turning the duck over every 30 minutes.

To make the mandarin sauce, heat a saucepan over high heat and add the stock. Boil rapidly for 3 minutes, or until the stock has reduced by half.

Squeeze the juice from the mandarin halves straight into the saucepan, then add the squeezed halves to the pan as well. (The natural pectin in the mandarins will give the sauce a beautiful glossiness.) Reduce the heat to medium and boil for another 5 minutes, then remove from the heat and season to taste with salt.

Remove the duck from the oven, cover lightly with foil and leave to rest for 5–10 minutes.

To serve, pour the sauce through a fine-meshed sieve into a clean saucepan. Add the mandarin segments and warm the sauce through gently over medium heat for about 3 minutes.

Carve the duck into 6–8 pieces and serve with the mandarin sauce.

VEAL COTOLETTA
◇ WITH ◇
SMASHED PUMPKIN AND MARINATED ZUCCHINI

My fondest memory of eating out as a child was Sunday lunch with my maternal grandparents at the Transylvania. This old restaurant in the Melbourne suburb of Prahran was where you went for the best beef goulash and veal schnitzels that covered the entire plate. My veal cotoletta are more refined but no less satisfying. Cooper's bar mitzvah was Italian themed and the men couldn't believe their luck when these oversized chops appeared on their plates.

SERVES 6

200 g (7 oz) breadcrumbs
zest of 1 lemon
1 teaspoon salt
1 teaspoon pepper
50 g (1¾ oz/⅓ cup) plain (all-purpose) flour
3 eggs, beaten
6 × 220 g (8 oz) veal cutlets, French trimmed
olive oil, for frying

Smashed pumpkin
125 ml (4 fl oz/½ cup) olive oil
1 kg (2 lb 3 oz) butternut or jap pumpkin, cut into
   2 cm (¾ in) cubes
2 garlic cloves, finely sliced
5 sprigs flat-leaf (Italian) parsley, plus 1 tablespoon
   chopped
2 teaspoons salt

Marinated zucchini
6–8 small zucchinis (courgettes)
1 tablespoon salt
1 garlic clove, finely chopped
125 ml (4 fl oz/½ cup) olive oil
4 tablespoons balsamic vinegar
3 tablespoons finely chopped mint
1 tablespoon pine nuts

Combine the breadcrumbs, lemon zest, salt and pepper in a shallow bowl. Put the flour in a second bowl, and the beaten egg in a third bowl.

One by one, coat the veal cutlets first in the flour, shaking off any excess, then dip them in the beaten egg, and finally coat them in the breadcrumb mixture. Place the crumbed cutlets on a baking tray.

To make the smashed pumpkin, heat the oil in a large saucepan over low heat. Add the pumpkin, garlic, parsley sprigs and salt. Cover with a lid and cook for 10 minutes, stirring occasionally, until the pumpkin breaks down to a rough consistency.

Remove the pumpkin from the heat and stir. Check and adjust the seasoning if necessary, then sprinkle with the chopped parsley and keep warm until ready to serve.

To prepare the marinated zucchini, shave the zucchinis lengthways with a potato peeler or on a mandoline. Put the zucchini ribbons in a bowl, sprinkle over the salt and toss well. Allow to sit for 1 hour so the salt draws out the moisture, then drain. Transfer to a serving bowl and add the remaining ingredients. Mix gently to combine.

Heat 3–4 tablespoons of oil in a large frying pan over medium heat. Cook the cutlets, in batches, for 3 minutes each side for medium, or until cooked to your liking.

Serve the cutlets hot with the smashed pumpkin and marinated zucchini on the side.

MISS RUBEN'S PASTRAMI

——— ◇ ———

If cooking is the way to a man's heart, then our pastrami is a direct injection. I've had marriage proposals over Miss Ruben's pastrami. It's a three-day process for us, but this recipe reduces the steps and cooking time so you can easily make it at home (although the sauerkraut still needs to be made five days in advance). Serve the pastrami warm, piled on rye bread with pickles, sauerkraut and mustard, or with potato salad, slaw and all the trimmings. You won't be disappointed.

SERVES 6-8

1 tablespoon black peppercorns
1 tablespoon white peppercorns
1½ tablespoons coriander seeds
3 teaspoons cumin seeds
1 tablespoon light brown sugar
2 teaspoons salt
1.5 kg (3 lb 5 oz) pickled beef brisket
2 tablespoons American mustard
pickled cucumbers, to serve
rye bread, to serve
mustard of your choice, to serve

Red sauerkraut
1 medium red cabbage, about 1 kg (2 lb 3 oz),
   finely shredded
1 teaspoon rock salt
2 teaspoons caraway seeds
¼ bay leaf
1 juniper berry

To make the sauerkraut, put the cabbage in a large bowl. Using a spice grinder, blend together the rock salt, caraway seeds, bay leaf and juniper berry. Sprinkle the salt mix over the cabbage and massage well until the cabbage has softened. Cover with plastic wrap and leave to stand overnight at room temperature.

The next day, massage the cabbage again and transfer it with its liquid to a sealed airtight container.

Leave the sauerkraut to ferment for 5 days at room temperature, opening the container to air for a few minutes every couple of days. Transfer it to the refrigerator to stop the fermenting process.

Preheat the oven to 170°C (340°F).

Grind the peppercorns, coriander and cumin seeds in a spice grinder or mortar and pestle. Mix with the sugar and salt.

Using a pastry brush, spread the brisket with mustard, then sprinkle with the spice mix, ensuring the meat is evenly coated.

Place the brisket on a wire rack set over a roasting tray. Roast in the oven for 4½ hours. Wait for it to cool slightly before slicing thickly.

Serve the pastrami sliced and still warm, thickly layered on top of the sauerkraut and pickled cucumber, between slices of rye bread with mustard.

Note: You should be able to order pickled beef brisket through your butcher.

BEEF AND LAMB KOFTAS
◇ WITH ◇
MANGO SALSA

Grilling meats on horizontal skewers has an ancient history in the Eastern Mediterranean and was likely brought to Australia by Lebanese immigrants. It's believed that this is how the Hebrews cooked in the wilderness during the Exodus from Egypt. These koftas are even better when cooked on the barbecue. Serve them wrapped in warm pittas with salad, hummus and this delicious mango salsa.

SERVES 6

500 g (1 lb 2 oz) minced (ground) beef
500 g (1 lb 2 oz) minced (ground) lamb
2 teaspoons sweet paprika
2 teaspoons smoked paprika
2 teaspoons ground coriander
2 teaspoons ground cumin
2 teaspoons ground cinnamon
3 teaspoons salt
pinch of freshly cracked black pepper
60 g (2 oz) pine nuts
20 g (¾ oz/1 cup) flat-leaf (Italian) parsley,
   chopped
1 tablespoon olive oil

12 bamboo skewers, soaked in water for at least
   2 hours

Mango salsa
1 whole large mango, pit removed and cut into
   1 cm (½ in) cubes
1½ green chillies, seeded and finely diced
½ red onion, finely diced
½ cucumber, seeds removed and cut into 5 mm
   (¼ in) cubes
2 tablespoons finely chopped coriander (cilantro)
   leaves
zest and juice of 1 lime
2 tablespoons olive oil
sea salt and freshly cracked black pepper, to taste

Preheat the oven to 180°C (350°F).

To make the kofta mixture, combine the minced beef and lamb, the spices, salt, pepper, pine nuts and parsley in a medium bowl. Mix well. Divide the kofta mixture into 12 portions.

To make the koftas, take a portion of the mixture and pierce it with a skewer. With wet hands, work the meat up the skewer to create a log shape about 12.5–15 cm (5–6 in) long, squeezing tightly. Make a few dents in the kofta with your finger. Repeat with the rest of the mixture to make 12 koftas.

Heat the oil in a large chargrill or frying pan over medium–high heat. Working in batches, add the koftas to the pan and cook for 3 minutes, turning regularly to brown all sides. Transfer the koftas to a baking tray lined with baking paper.

Cook the koftas in the oven for 8 minutes, ensuring they are still slightly pink in the middle.

To make the mango salsa, combine all the ingredients in a mixing bowl and season to taste with salt and pepper.

Serve the koftas hot with the mango salsa on the side.

STICKY BEEF RIBS
◇

This is one of those dishes you'll make time and time again. It's pure comfort food, and needs nothing more than some Greens with chilli and garlic (page 174) and Spiced coconut rice (page 166) for a guaranteed crowd-pleasing meal. Make sure you marinate the ribs overnight for best results. If you can manage it, try to leave some leftovers to make Sticky beef fried rice (page 134).

SERVES 6-8

2 kg (4 lb 6 oz) beef spare ribs

Marinade
1 tablespoon black peppercorns
pinch of whole cloves
2 green cardamom pods
pinch of fenugreek seeds
3 teaspoons cumin seeds
1 teaspoon fennel seeds
1 star anise
2 cinnamon sticks
pinch of ground nutmeg
pinch of ground ginger
1¼ tablespoons sweet paprika
1 tablespoon sumac
1¼ tablespoons salt
125 ml (4 fl oz/½ cup) grapeseed oil
1 teaspoon fresh ginger, grated
2 garlic cloves, crushed
1 handful coriander (cilantro) leaves and stems, chopped, to serve

Honey glaze
juice of ½ lemon
90 g (3 oz/¼ cup) honey
45 g (1½ oz/¼ cup) light brown sugar
60 ml (2 fl oz/¼ cup) maple syrup

To make the marinade, toast the peppercorns, cloves, cardamom pods, fenugreek seeds, cumin seeds, fennel seeds, star anise and cinnamon stick in a large frying pan over medium–high heat for 2 minutes. Watch them carefully to ensure they don't burn.

Add the nutmeg, ginger, smoked paprika, sumac and salt, then transfer to a mortar and pestle or a spice grinder and grind to a powder.

In a bowl, combine the powdered spices with the remaining marinade ingredients, except the coriander.

Place the beef ribs in a roasting tray and rub all over with the marinade. Cover with foil and leave to marinate in the refrigerator overnight.

Preheat the oven to 150°C (300°F).

Roast the ribs in the oven for 4½ hours, until the meat is tender. After 1 hour, add 250 ml (8½ fl oz/1 cup) boiling water to the roasting tray and mix it with the pan juices. Baste the meat all over, then continue to baste with the juices once every hour.

Remove the beef ribs from the oven and increase the oven temperature to 250°C (480°F). Drain, and reserve the left-over beef cooking liquid if you are making the Sticky beef rib fried rice (page 134).

To make the honey glaze, combine all the ingredients in a bowl and mix well. Pour the honey glaze over the ribs, ensuring they are evenly coated. Return to the oven and continue to roast for approximately 20 minutes, basting every 5 minutes until sticky.

Transfer the ribs to a platter, pour over the pan juices and scatter with the chopped coriander to serve.

STICKY BEEF RIB FRIED RICE

◇

It's worth making extra Sticky beef ribs (page 133) so you can experience this dish. I served it at a cocktail party recently in baby bowls topped with a super cute fried quail egg. The chargrilled pineapple is delicious and can be done on a barbecue, but if you just want to curl up on the couch, then a generous squeeze of lime will do the trick in adding a fresh twist. The rice needs to be cooked the day before.

SERVES 6

55 g (2 oz/1 cup) coconut flakes
300 g (10½ oz) Sticky beef ribs (page 133)
125 ml (4 fl oz/½ cup) left-over beef cooking liquid (see method page 133)
2 tablespoons olive oil
3 eggs
½ fresh pineapple, cut into wedges
sea salt and freshly cracked black pepper, to taste
chilli hair, to garnish

Chipotle rice
660 g (1 lb 7 oz/3 cups) short-grain rice
60 ml (2 fl oz/¼ cup) rice bran oil
¼ onion, diced
200 g (7 oz) carrots, diced
100 g (3½ oz) peas
100 g (3½ oz) corn kernels
2 teaspoons chipotle in adobo sauce

Prepare the rice a day ahead. Wash and rinse the rice, then place in a rice cooker with 500 ml (17 fl oz/2 cups) water. Cook for 10–15 minutes, or until al dente. Spread the rice on a baking tray and leave to cool overnight in the refrigerator.

Preheat the oven to 170°C (340°F).

Heat the rice bran oil in a wok over medium heat. Add the onions and stir-fry until soft. Add the carrots and cook for 3 minutes. Add the rice, peas, corn and chipotle and cook for 5 minutes, stirring continuously, until heated through.

Spread the coconut flakes on a baking tray lined with baking paper, then transfer to the oven and toast for 3–4 minutes, tossing halfway through. Keep an eye on the flakes as they can burn easily.

Pull the beef off the bone and add to a saucepan with the left-over beef cooking liquid. Place over a medium heat and warm through until hot.

Add the beef and sauce to the fried rice, mixing gently to avoid breaking the meat up too much. Remove from the heat and keep warm.

Heat the oil in a non-stick frying pan over medium heat. Fry the eggs for about 3 minutes, until crisp on the edges. Remove and drain on paper towel.

Heat a chargrill pan over high heat until smoking hot. Place the pineapple wedges, flesh-side down, in the pan and grill for 2 minutes on each side, until juicy and charred.

Transfer the fried rice to a platter and top with the fried eggs. Season to taste with salt and pepper and garnish with the toasted coconut flakes and chilli hair.

Serve with charred pineapple wedges on the side.

Note: Chilli hair is available from specialty food stores.

12-HOUR LAMB SHOULDER

——— ◇ ———

This is a foolproof dish for even the most nervous cooks and makes for a wonderful dinner when you just want to put something in the oven and forget about it – all the preparation is done the day before. You should end up with meat that is tasty, succulent and tender. Cut through the richness of the lamb by serving it with some Chargrilled broccolini with green tahini (page 175). Ras el hanout is a North African spice mix.

SERVES 6-8

2.5 kg (5½ lb) lamb shoulder, semi-boned
2 tablespoons sea salt
60 ml (2 fl oz/¼ cup) extra-virgin olive oil
3 medium carrots, cut in half crossways
1 fennel bulb, quartered
1 garlic bulb, halved
1 red onion, peeled and cut in half lengthways
1 preserved lemon, halved
135 g (5 oz) honey
500 ml (17 fl oz/2 cups) chicken stock
Chargrilled broccolini with green tahini, to serve (page 175)

Ras el hanout
60 g (2 oz/½ cup) cumin seeds
20 g (¾ oz/¼ cup) coriander seeds
1 tablespoon black peppercorns
1 tablespoon chilli flakes
5 tablespoons smoked paprika
2 tablespoons ground cinnamon
½ teaspoon ground allspice
pinch of freshly grated nutmeg

To make the ras el hanout, toast the cumin and coriander seeds in a frying pan over medium heat until fragrant. Using a spice grinder or mortar and pestle, grind them finely, then grind the black peppercorns. Mix the ground spices with the remaining ingredients in a small bowl.

Place the lamb shoulder in a large roasting tin, at least 5 cm (2 in) deep. Rub the salt and oil over the lamb and massage in 50 g (1¾ oz/½ cup) of the ras el hanout.

Distribute the vegetables, garlic, onion and preserved lemon under and around the meat. Cover and refrigerate overnight. Remove the meat from the fridge at least 1 hour before you want to cook it (roughly 12 hours before you want to eat it).

Preheat the oven to 200°C (400°F).

Smear the meat with half the honey, reserving the rest. Add the stock to the roasting tray and seal with a double layer of foil.

Roast the shoulder in the oven for 20 minutes, then reduce the temperature to 100°C (210°F) and slow-roast for a further 10–12 hours, until the meat is falling off the bone.

Remove the lamb from the oven and leave to cool a little before straining the pan juices into a saucepan. Reserve the roasted vegetables to serve with the lamb or discard.

Once the pan juices have cooled, skim off any fat from the surface and place the saucepan over medium heat. Add the remaining honey and boil for about 10–15 minutes, or until slightly reduced.

Pour the jus over the lamb and return the tray to the oven uncovered for 15 minutes, until a slight crust forms and the lamb is warm. Remove it from the oven and allow it to cool slightly.

Pile the roasted vegetables, if using, onto a serving platter and place the lamb on top. Drizzle with the sauce and serve with the chargrilled broccolini.

POACHED VEAL
—◇ WITH ◇—
SAFFRON AIOLI AND QUAIL EGGS

This is my take on the lovely Italian dish vitello tonnato for those who don't eat meat and fish on the same plate. Poaching results in moist, tender meat. The saffron aioli, cornichons and crispy capers add delicious sharp flavours, and the quail eggs make it shine. Note that you need to poach the veal the night before. Serve it on a platter as part of a grazing table or individually plated up.

SERVES 8–10

1 kg (2 lb 3 oz) veal girello
6 quail eggs
30 g (1 oz/1 cup) celery heart leaves
10 cornichons, to garnish
sea salt and freshly cracked black pepper, to taste
Raw greens and grains (page 93), to serve

Court boullion
2 garlic cloves
2 carrots, sliced
1 onion, chopped
3 celery stalks, chopped
1 leek, white part only, sliced
6 juniper berries
6 peppercorns
3 thyme sprigs
1 bay leaf

Saffron aioli
2 eggs
½ teaspoon saffron threads
250 ml (8½ fl oz/1 cup) grapeseed oil
1 garlic clove, retrieved from the court bouillon once the veal has cooked, crushed

Crispy capers
1 tablespoon olive oil, plus extra for drizzling
50 g (1¾ oz) capers

To make the court bouillon, combine all the ingredients in a large saucepan with 4 litres (135 fl oz/16 cups) water. Bring to the boil for 10 minutes.

Add the veal to the court bouillon and poach for 1 hour over low heat, until the internal temperature of the meat reaches 50°C (122°F) when tested with a sugar thermometer.

Remove from the heat and retrieve the garlic clove for the saffron aioli. Refrigerate the veal in the court boullion overnight.

To make the aioli, combine all the ingredients in a small jug. Using a hand-held blender, gently pulse to blend the ingredients until smooth and emulsified.

Half-fill a small saucepan with water and bring to the boil. Gently add the quail eggs and boil for 3 minutes. Drain, refresh under cold water, then peel and rinse the eggs. Cut in half.

Pick the celery leaves and immerse in cold water until ready to serve.

For the crispy capers, heat the oil in a small frying pan over high heat. Fry the capers for about 1 minute, or until crispy. Drain on paper towel and season with salt.

To serve, drain the celery leaves and the veal, discarding the court boullion. Slice the veal into 3 mm (⅛ in) slices and arrange on a platter. Top with the eggs, celery leaves, cornichons and crispy capers. Fill a piping (icing) bag with the saffron aioli and pipe it in small dollops all over the veal. Season well with salt and pepper, and finish with a drizzle of oil. Serve with the raw greens salad on the side.

OSSO BUCCO

——◇ WITH ◇——

PRUNES, SHALLOTS AND BLOOD ORANGE GREMOLATA

Prunes and golden shallots add a subtle sweetness to this dish. It's actually better made the day before you want to eat it because it gives the flavours time to develop. You can mix any left-over spätzle with butter and parsley as a side to fish.

SERVES 6

35 g (1¼ oz/¼ cup) plain (all-purpose) flour
2 teaspoons ground allspice
2 kg (4 lb 6 oz) osso bucco
75 ml (2½ fl oz) olive oil, plus extra for drizzling
7 large French shallots, halved
2 celery stalks, roughly chopped
6 garlic cloves, crushed
250 ml (8½ fl oz/1 cup) red wine
250 g (9 oz) tomato passata (puréed tomatoes)
500 ml (17 fl oz/2 cups) chicken stock
200 g (7 oz) prunes, pitted
12 Dutch carrots, ends trimmed
1 bay leaf
2 cinnamon sticks

Spätzle
300 g (10½ oz/2 cups) plain (all-purpose) flour
5 eggs
60 ml (2 fl oz/¼ cup) almond, soy or cow's milk
sea salt and ground white pepper, for seasoning

Blood orange gremolata
zest of 1 blood orange
zest of 1 lemon
3 garlic cloves, finely chopped
2 tablespoons finely chopped flat-leaf (Italian)
  parsley

Preheat the oven to 150°C (300°F).

Combine the flour and allspice on a plate. Coat the meat in the flour mixture until fully coated, shaking off any excess, and transfer to a plate.

Heat most of the oil in a large, heavy-based cast-iron pot over medium heat. Sear the meat, working in batches, until golden brown on both sides. Set aside.

Add a splash more oil to the pot, then add the shallots and celery. Fry, stirring regularly, for about 8 minutes, until soft and golden. Add the garlic and cook for 5 minutes.

Return the meat to the pot, add the red wine, and simmer for 2–3 minutes. Add the tomato passata, chicken stock, prunes, carrots, bay leaf and cinnamon sticks. Bring to the boil, then reduce the heat to medium and cover with a lid.

Transfer the pot to the oven and cook for approximately 4 hours, until the meat is falling off the bone.

To make the gremolata, combine all the ingredients in a a small bowl.

To make the spätzle, mix together all the ingredients in a bowl. Fill a saucepan with salted water and bring to the boil. Pass the spätzle mixture through a spätzle-maker, a potato ricer fitted with a wide-gauge plate, or a colander, into the boiling water. Cook for 3 minutes, then drain.

To serve, divide the spätzle among the bowls and drizzle with oil. Top with the osso bucco and scatter over the gremolata to finish.

SIDES

WHOLE ROASTED CAULIFLOWER
— ◇ — WITH — ◇ —
TAHINI AND TOMATO SALSA

Cauliflower is probably my favourite vegetable and I could eat it cooked like this every day. One of my chefs, Matthew Wihongi, created this recipe for our catering business and it really wows. If you don't have time to slow roast the cauli, parboil it until it is soft enough to pierce with a fork. Then put it in the oven with the saffron liquid and baste until golden.

SERVES 4-6

1 large cauliflower head
1 tablespoon saffron threads
1 tablespoon sumac
1 teaspoon ground turmeric
1 teaspoon ground cumin
1 teaspoon ground coriander
½ teaspoon ground chilli
90 ml (3 fl oz) olive oil, plus extra if needed
1 teaspoon salt
540 g (1 lb 3 oz/2 cups) Tahini dip (page 31), to serve
80 g (2¾ oz/½ cup) slivered pistachios, to garnish
2 tablespoons pomegranate seeds, to garnish
2 tablespoons chilli hair, to garnish

Tomato salsa
¼ red onion, finely diced
5 tomatoes, deseeded and finely diced
2 tablespoons chopped coriander (cilantro) leaves
2 teaspoons olive oil
2 teaspoons lemon juice
sea salt, to taste

Preheat the oven to 180°C (350°F).

Place the cauliflower head on a baking tray lined with baking paper.

Combine the saffron threads with 500 ml (17 fl oz/ 2 cups) boiling water and set aside to steep for 15–20 minutes.

In a bowl, combine the saffron liquid with the sumac, ground spices, oil and salt. Pour the mixture over the cauliflower, making sure it is evenly coated.

Cover the tray with foil and roast the cauliflower in the oven for 2 hours, basting every 30 minutes with the saffron liquid. Add more oil if needed to keep the cauliflower moist.

Remove the foil and roast for a further 10 minutes to brown the cauliflower a little.

While the cauliflower is browning, make the tomato salsa. Combine all the ingredients in a bowl and mix well. Season to taste with salt.

To serve, spread the tahini dip on a large platter and place the cauliflower on top. Cut out a generous wedge of cauliflower and pile the tomato salsa inside and around the edge of the cauliflower. Garnish with slivered pistachios, pomegranate seeds and chilli hair.

Note: Chilli hair is available from specialty food stores.

FRIED BREADED CAULIFLOWER

◇

This recipe is one of my childhood favourites. Adjust the seasoning in the breadcrumbs to suit your taste and serve hot as a snack, or as a side to meat dishes such as Brined roast chicken with chimichurri (page 117).

SERVES 4-6

1 small cauliflower head, broken into florets
2 eggs, beaten
80 g (2¾ oz/1 cup) fresh breadcrumbs
1 teaspoon sea salt, plus extra to taste
¼ teaspoon chilli flakes
¼ teaspoon dried dill
¼ teaspoon freshly cracked black pepper
olive oil, for shallow-frying

Half-fill a saucepan with salted water and bring to the boil. Add the cauliflower florets reduce the heat to medium–high and simmer for 6–8 minutes, or until the cauliflower is just tender. Drain and set aside to cool slightly.

Put the beaten eggs in a bowl. Combine the breadcrumbs in a shallow bowl with the rest of the dry ingredients.

Dip the florets first in the beaten egg, then coat them with the breadcrumb mixture, shaking off any excess. Transfer the crumbed cauliflower to a baking tray.

Heat about 5 cm (2 in) of oil in a large heavy-based frying pan over medium–high heat. Carefully fry the florets, in batches if necessary, for 2–3 minutes on each side, until golden brown. Transfer to a wire rack with paper towel underneath to catch any excess oil. Sprinkle with salt, to taste.

GUACAMOLE
—◇ WITH ◇—
CHARGRILLED
CORN SALSA

The chargrilled corn in this guacamole lifts everyone's favourite dip to a whole new level.

SERVES 6-8

Guacamole
4 large ripe avocados
1 large French shallot, finely diced
½ small bunch coriander (cilantro) leaves and
   soft stalks, finely shredded, plus extra sprigs
   to garnish
½ long green chilli, seeded and finely diced
1 teaspoon ground cumin
1 teaspoon ground coriander
juice of 2 limes, plus extra to taste
2 teaspoons sea salt, plus extra to taste
crackers, to serve
lime wedges, to serve

Chargrilled corn salsa
2 corn cobs, husks removed
2 tablespoons pepitas (pumpkin seeds)
½ teaspoon sweet paprika
½ small red onion, finely sliced
1 tablespoon olive oil
1 teaspoon lemon juice
½ teaspoon sea salt
½ teaspoon ground cumin

To make the guacamole, halve the avocados and remove the stones. Scoop the flesh into a bowl and mash well, leaving some chunks for texture. Add all the other ingredients and mix well. Taste for seasoning and tang, and add extra salt and lime juice if necessary.

To make the chargrilled corn salsa, heat a chargrill pan over high heat. Grill the corn cobs, turning regularly, until nicely charred. Leave to cool, then cut the kernals from the cobs.

Heat a frying pan over medium heat and toast the pepitas for 5 minutes, or until golden.

Combine the rest of the salsa ingredients in a bowl, then add the charred corn and pepitas. Mix well.

To serve, spoon the guacamole into a serving bowl and pile the chargrilled corn salsa on top. Garnish with extra coriander sprigs and serve with crackers and lime wedges.

Pictured on page 150.

POTATO AND CARROT LATKE
— ◇ WITH ◇ —
HERBY QUARK
AND SALMON EGGS

These oversized latke are a grown-up version of the ones I ate every year to celebrate Chanukah. They were a particular favourite of my dad and brother. My family are salt addicts – no matter how good the latke tasted, we would always sprinkle each with salt before eating it. We could often demolish more than twenty in one sitting.

SERVES 8

3 potatoes, peeled and cut in half
½ carrot, peeled
3 tablespoons chopped dill, plus extra sprigs to garnish
2 tablespoons potato starch
1 egg
1½ teaspoons salt
½ teaspoon freshly cracked black pepper
3 tablespoons olive oil
1 tablespoon salmon eggs, to garnish

Herby quark
350 g (12½ oz) quark
1 tablespoon finely chopped dill
1 tablespoon finely chopped flat-leaf (Italian) parsley
1 tablespoon finely chopped chives
1 teaspoon lemon juice
2 tablespoons olive oil

Place the potatoes in a large saucepan and cover with cold water. Bring to the boil, then take off the heat and drain. The potatoes need to be solid enough to grate, so they need very little cooking.

When the potatoes are cool enough to handle, grate them into a mixing bowl. Grate the carrot into the bowl also.

Add the chopped dill, potato starch, egg, salt and pepper, and mix well.

Heat the oil in 2 × 20 cm (8 in) frying pans over very high heat, then put half the mixture in each pan, flattening them down well.

Brown the latke for 30 seconds on each side, then reduce the heat to low and continue cooking for a further 10 minutes on each side.

To make the herby quark, combine all the ingredients in a bowl and mix well.

Serve the latke warm, topped with spoonfuls of herby quark, with salmon eggs and dill sprigs to garnish.

MIXED MUSHROOM
◇ AND ◇
QUINOA PILAF

The combination of different mushrooms, as well as the pilaf cooking technique, turns bland quinoa into an earthy, ultra-flavoursome side dish that can really be served on its own. Turn leftovers into brekkie by topping with a poached egg.

SERVES 6-8

100 g (3½ oz) porcini mushrooms
200 g (7 oz) butter
90 ml (3 fl oz) olive oil, plus extra for frying
1 brown onion, finely diced
1 garlic clove, finely diced
250 g (9 oz/1¼ cups) black quinoa
250 g (9 oz/1¼ cups) white quinoa
500 g (1 lb 2 oz) Swiss brown mushrooms
200 g (7 oz) enoki mushrooms
250 g (9 oz) button mushrooms
1 litre (34 fl oz/4 cups) chicken stock, plus extra
  if needed
1 teaspoon salt
¼ teaspoon freshly cracked black pepper

Soak the porcini mushrooms in 250 ml (8½ fl oz/ 1 cup) boiling water and set aside for 20 minutes, then finely chop.

Heat the butter and oil in a large saucepan over medium heat. Add the onion and garlic and cook for 10 minutes. Add both the black and white quinoa and cook for a further 10 minutes, until the quinoa starts to brown and forms a crisp crust.

Meanwhile, finely chop the remaining mushrooms, reserving a few whole mushrooms to be sautéed and used as garnish.

Add the chopped mushrooms (including the porcini) and the chicken stock to the quinoa and mix well. Cover the saucepan with foil and then the lid. Cook for 15 minutes, then check the liquid hasn't reduced too much. Top up with a little more stock if necessary. Give it a good stir and cook for another 15 minutes.

Remove the quinoa from the heat and stir again. Cover with the foil and leave to rest for 5 minutes. Add the salt and pepper, and mix well.

While the quinoa is resting, add 1 tablespoon of oil to a frying pan and place over medium heat. Sauté the reserved whole mushrooms for about 10 minutes, until brown.

Transfer the quinoa to a serving bowl and sprinkle with the whole sautéed mushrooms to finish.

SPICED ISRAELI COUSCOUS

◇

A tasty side dish that goes well with just about anything: try Fish stew with turmeric aioli (page 115) or any meat dish.

SERVES 4-6

50 ml (1¾ fl oz) grapeseed oil
1 large onion, finely diced
1 garlic clove, crushed
zest of 2 lemons
pinch of dried chilli flakes
60 g (1 oz/½ cup) green sultanas (golden raisins)
pinch of saffron threads, soaked in 1 tablespoon tepid water
juice of 1 orange
1½ teaspoons sweet smoked paprika
250 g (9 oz/1⅓ cups) couscous
625 ml (21 fl oz/2½ cups) chicken stock or water

Heat the oil a large saucepan over medium–low heat. Add the onion, garlic, lemon zest, chilli flakes and sultanas. Sweat for 20 minutes, stirring occasionally, until the onion is soft and golden. Add the saffron in its soaking water, along with the orange juice and paprika. Cook for another 5 minutes.

Pour the chicken stock or water into a small saucepan and bring to the boil.

Mix the couscous into the onion mixture, then add the boiling chicken stock or water. Cover the pan with a lid, and continue cooking for 8–10 minutes, until the couscous is fluffy and has absorbed almost all the liquid.

Remove from the heat and loosen the couscous with a fork.

EGG, SRIRACHA MAYO - 15
• BAGEL - TOASTED w̄ HERBY QUARK
& SALMON - 12

• SALAD
ADD

CHOCOLATE CHIP
& TAHINI
COOKIES

RYE BREAD

—◇—

This really dark and slightly sweet rye bread makes amazing crisps when thinly sliced and toasted – they're the perfect accompaniment to Hummus (page 32) or Golden beetroot tahini (page 31).

MAKES 2 LOAVES

2 tablespoons dried yeast
2 tablespoons caster (superfine) sugar
450 g (1 lb/4½ cups) rye flour
1 kg (2 lb 3 oz/6⅔ cups) plain (all-purpose) flour, plus extra for dusting
200 g (7 oz) spelt flour
200 g (7 oz) light brown sugar
3 tablespoons Dutch (unsweetened) cocoa powder
20 g (¾ oz/¼ cup) coffee powder
30 g (1 oz/⅓ cup) fennel seed powder
225 g (8 oz) molasses

Mix the yeast and sugar in a bowl with 975 g (2 lb 2 oz) warm water. Allow to sit for around 10 minutes to activate the yeast. It should appear foamy.

Combine all of the dry ingredients in the bowl of a stand mixer fitted with the dough hook attachment.

Stir the molasses through the yeast mixture and pour it into the dry ingredients. Mix until a dough forms.

Turn the dough out onto a floured work surface and knead until smooth and elastic. Divide the mixture in half and shape to place into two 20 × 12 cm (8 × 4¾ in) loaf (bar) tins.

Cover the tins with a damp tea towel (dish towel) and leave the dough to prove in a warm place for about 1 hour, or until it has doubled in size.

Preheat the oven to 200°C (400°F).

Bake the loaves in the oven for 1 hour. Remove from the oven and allow the loaves to cool in the tin. Turn them out and slice as needed.

Note: It's important to weigh the water in this recipe to get an exact measurement.

To make dark rye crisps, preheat the oven to 160°C (320°F).

Once the loaves have cooled, slice one loaf into wafer-thin slices using a bread knife or an electric knife and lay out as a single layer on a lined baking tray. Toast in the oven until very crisp, about 10 minutes, turning once. Do not allow the toasts to colour further.

SPICE-ROASTED SWEET POTATO
◇ WITH ◇
SHANKLISH, DATES AND PICKLED SHALLOTS

I'd never tried roasted dates until creating this recipe and I'm so glad I did. To get the best result it's really worth buying fresh medjool dates for their juiciness. The flavours of date molasses, lime and fresh white cheese are so good with the caramelised roasted sweet potato. You can buy shanklish from Middle Eastern grocers, otherwise feta or fresh ricotta would also be delicious.

SERVES 6-8

2 kg (4 lb 6 oz) sweet potato, peeled and cut into 6 cm (2½ in) wedges
2 tablespoons white sesame seeds
2 tablespoons cumin seeds
3 tablespoons olive oil
sea salt, for seasoning
10 medjool dates, sliced into thirds and stones removed
150 g (5½ oz) white shanklish or other soft white cheese
red chilli, sliced, to garnish
coriander (cilantro) sprigs, to garnish

Pickled red shallots
100 ml (3½ fl oz) red wine vinegar
1 tablespoon, plus 1 teaspoon caster (superfine) sugar
¾ tablespoon salt
4 red shallots, thinly sliced

Dressing
juice of 1 lime
2 tablespoons date molasses
2 tablespoons extra-virgin olive oil
1 teaspoon sea salt

Preheat the oven to 200°C (400°F) and line two baking trays with baking paper.

In a bowl, toss the sweet potato wedges with the seeds and oil and season with salt, then place the wedges on the prepared trays.

Roast in the oven for 25–30 minutes, until the edges of the potato are brown and the flesh is soft.

Line another baking tray with baking paper and spread the date pieces on top. Roast the dates in the oven for 6 minutes, then remove and leave to cool and crisp up.

To make the pickled red shallots, combine the vinegar, sugar and salt with 250 ml (8½ fl oz/1 cup) water in a saucepan. Bring to the boil, then leave to simmer for 3–4 minutes before removing from the heat.

Place the shallots in a bowl and pour the hot pickling liquid over them. Leave to sit for 1 hour before serving.

To make the dressing whisk together all the ingredients in a bowl.

To serve, arrange the sweet potato wedges on a platter, crumble over the shanklish in big chunks, then top with the roasted dates and pickled red shallots.

Drizzle with the dressing and garnish with the sliced chilli and coriander.

SICILIAN BRAISED FENNEL
◇ WITH ◇
CARROT AND ORANGE

Some of the most iconic Italian foods have their origins in the Jewish communities of Italy. For nearly 2000 years the most vibrant Jewish communities were found on the island of Sicily. The braised fennel in this Sicilian-inspired side dish really takes on the flavour of the orange. It's a great accompaniment to meat or fish, and is especially good on a hot summer day.

SERVES 6-8

90 ml (3 fl oz) olive oil
2 medium garlic cloves, thinly sliced
2 carrots, coarsely grated
4 medium fennel bulbs, sliced into 1 cm (½ in) lengths
125 ml (4 fl oz/1 cup) white wine
250 ml (8½ fl oz/1 cup) chicken or vegetable stock
3 strips of zest and juice of 1 orange
½ teaspoon fennel seeds
5 thyme sprigs, plus extra thyme leaves to garnish
¼ teaspoon caster (superfine) sugar
1½ teaspoon salt flakes
freshly ground black pepper, for seasoning

Heat 2 tablespoons of the oil in a large pot and sauté the garlic over medium heat for 1 minute.

Add the grated carrot and cook for 3 minutes until softened, then set aside.

Heat another 2 tablespoons of the oil in a large frying pan, place half the fennel slices in the pan and brown over medium heat until caramelised, around 3 minutes. Repeat with the remaining oil and fennel.

Add the caramelised fennel to the pot with the carrots and garlic. Add the wine, stock, orange zest and juice and adjust heat to a simmer. Then add the fennel seeds, thyme sprigs and sugar, and season with salt and pepper.

Stir gently with a wooden spoon and cook until the liquid has reduced and is syrupy, and the fennel is tender, around 10 minutes.

Place the mixture in a large serving bowl and sprinkle extra thyme leaves on top. Serve warm or at room temperature.

Pictured on page 160.

ROASTED DUTCH CARROTS
◇ WITH ◇
HONEY AND CUMIN

I'm a real savoury kind of girl, so tzimmes – a sweet stew made from carrots, dried fruits and honey and typically served at Rosh Hashanah – isn't for me. I am, however, very partial to these honey-roasted Dutch carrots strewn with cumin seeds.

SERVES 4-6

115 g (4 oz/⅓ cup) honey
80 ml (2½ fl oz/⅓ cup) olive oil
2 tablespoons cumin seeds
sea salt and freshly cracked black pepper,
    for seasoning
24 Dutch carrots, peeled

Preheat the oven to 200°C (400°F).

Mix the honey, oil and cumin seeds in a large bowl, and season generously with salt and pepper.

Add the carrots to the honey mixture, tossing to coat well, then transfer to a roasting tray.

Roast in the oven for 1 hour and 15 minutes, until golden brown, mixing halfway through.

Pictured on page 161.

BRAISED ARTICHOKES
◇ WITH ◇
WHITE WINE AND THYME

Artichokes are my second favourite vegetable, after cauliflower, and I think they are totally misunderstood. Most people I know wouldn't attempt to cook them in any shape or form, but they don't know what they're missing out on! Artichokes are actually quite forgiving once you've removed the outer leaves and covered them in lemony water to stop them oxidising. This dish is a great place to start – by braising the artichokes they take on the flavours of wine, butter and thyme, with beautiful results.

SERVES 6-8

8 artichokes, stems and outer leaves removed
juice of 2½ lemons
60 ml (2 fl oz/¼ cup) grapeseed oil
2 garlic cloves, crushed
6 thyme sprigs
50 g (1¾ oz) butter
375 ml (12½ fl oz/1½ cups) white wine
sea salt and freshly cracked black pepper, to taste

Preheat the oven to 170°C (340°F).

Cut the artichokes in half lengthways and remove the furry choke from the inside. Submerge in a bowl of iced water with the juice of half a lemon and set aside.

Heat the oil in a ovenproof pan over high heat. When the oil is hot, place the artichokes face-down in the pan.

Cook the artichokes for 5 minutes on each side, until brown. Watch them carefully to make sure they don't burn.

Add the garlic and thyme to the pan and stir for 2 minutes, then add the butter, wine and remaining lemon juice. Bring to a simmer, then cover with a lid and transfer to the oven to cook for 20 minutes.

Remove from the oven and season to taste with salt and pepper.

SUMAC
—◇ AND ◇—
POLENTA FRIED ARTICHOKES

These are an interpretation of the famous Italian-Jewish dish carciofi alla giudia, otherwise known as 'fried artichokes'. Serve them hot with a chilled glass of wine, or as part of a larger sharing table.

SERVES 4

4 eggs
375 g (13 oz/2½ cups) polenta
12 artichokes, stems on and outer leaves removed
250 ml (8½ fl oz/1 cup) vegetable oil
60 g (2 oz) sumac
sea salt and freshly cracked black pepper, to taste

Beat the eggs in one bowl and put the polenta in another bowl.

One at a time, dip the artichokes first in the egg, then coat in the polenta, shaking off any excess. Transfer to a baking tray.

Heat the oil in a cast-iron frying pan over high heat until smoking. Reduce the heat to medium.

Working in batches, shallow-fry the artichokes for about 4–5 minutes on each side, or until golden brown. Place on a wire rack with paper towel underneath to catch any excess oil.

While hot, sprinkle the artichoke with the sumac and season generously with salt and pepper.

Note: Ensure you use a cast-iron frying pan to lock in the heat.

SPICED COCONUT RICE
◇

Fragrant and fluffy, this simple rice is the perfect accompaniment to strongly flavoured meat and fish dishes such as Roast duck and mandarin sauce (page 125).

SERVES 6-8

600 g (1 lb 5 oz/3 cups) basmati rice
2 cinnamon sticks
6 cardamom pods
4 star anise
90 g (3 oz/1 cup) desiccated coconut

Rinse the rice in cold water, then drain and put in a large saucepan. Add the remaining ingredients, and mix well.

Add 1 litre (34 fl oz/4 cups) cold water, enough to cover the rice by 2 cm (¾ in), and bring to a rapid boil, then remove from the heat. Cover the rice with a damp tea towel (dish towel) and seal tightly with a lid.

Leave the rice to steam for 25 minutes, until any remaining liquid has absorbed and the rice is tender.

SAFFRON AND BARBERRY PILAF
◇

The rice vermicelli makes this pilaf that bit more interesting; feel free to also add nuts or dried mulberries. Serve with Pomegranate and honey-glazed poussin (page 120).

SERVES 6-8

1 teaspoon saffron threads
1 litre (34 fl oz/4 cups) chicken or vegetable stock
60 ml (2 fl oz/¼ cup) olive oil, plus extra for frying
½ onion, finely diced
1 garlic clove, crushed
1 teaspoon finely grated ginger
1 teaspoon ground cinnamon
1 teaspoon ground cumin
1 teaspoon ground coriander
1½ teaspoons sea salt
250 g (9 oz) rice vermicelli noodles, broken into bite-sized pieces
400 g (14 oz/2 cups) basmati rice, soaked overnight in cold water
4 tablespoons barberries
2 tablespoons chopped flat-leaf (Italian) parsley, to garnish

Combine the saffron threads and stock in a saucepan. Bring to a simmer over medium heat, then remove and set aside.

Heat the oil in a deep, heavy-based frying pan over medium heat and fry the onion, garlic and ginger for 5 minutes. Add the spices and salt and fry for 30 seconds, then add the rice noodles and fry until golden.

Drain the rice and add to the frying pan. Pour in the stock and bring to the boil. Reduce the heat to low, cover with a lid and cook for 10–12 minutes, or until the liquid is absorbed. Remove from the heat, take off the lid and place a clean tea towel (dish towel) over the rice. Leave to steam for a further 10–12 minutes.

Heat 1 tablespoon of oil in a small saucepan over medium heat. Fry the barberries for 30 seconds, then stir through the rice mixture with the parsley.

Pictured on page 120.

SPELT PITTAS

—◇—

With pitta bread so widely available, it's not something most people think to make. But they are really simple, and it's great fun to watch them pop open as they cook. Serve these immediately with Golden beetroot tahini (page 31) or Hummus (page 32), or warm gently in the oven before eating. Once cooked, the pittas should split easily to form pitta pockets.

SERVES 6–8

500 g (1 lb 2 oz/3⅓ cups) spelt flour, plus extra
   for dusting
2 teaspoons salt
1 teaspoon dried yeast

Mix the flour, salt and yeast with 330 g (11½ oz) water in the bowl of a stand mixer fitted with the dough hook attachment. Mix until a sticky dough forms, about 3–4 minutes.

Turn the dough out onto a floured surface and knead for 5–10 minutes, until the dough is smooth and elastic. Transfer to a lightly floured bowl, cover with a damp tea towel (dish towel) and leave to prove in a warm place for about 1 hour, or until the dough has doubled in size.

Turn the dough out onto a surface and punch it down to let the air out. Divide the dough into 50 g (1¾ oz) balls, or about 16 pieces, and place on a floured baking tray. Leave to rest for a further 10 minutes.

Heat a large frying pan over high heat.

Roll out each dough ball into 15 cm (6 in) rounds. Cook the pittas, one at a time, in the dry frying pan for 1 minute each side. They should puff up and look slightly scorched in places.

Serve the pittas warm.

Note: It's important to weigh the water in this recipe to get an exact measurement.

Pictured on page 30.

MILLA'S
◇ AND ◇
SEED CRACKERS

My twelve-year-old daughter, Milla, is an awesome cook. She makes a batch of these for us each week, adapted from a recipe she learnt from her school's kitchen garden program. These are delicious with anything from Hummus (page 32), to cheese, to Smoked white fish dip (page 34).

MAKES 16–20

60 g (2 oz/½ cup) sunflower seeds
40 g (1½ oz/¼ cup) linseeds (flax seeds)
2 tablespoons white sesame seeds
2 tablespoons black sesame seeds
2 tablespoons chia seeds
1 teaspoon sea salt, plus extra for seasoning
75 g (2¾ oz/½ cup) white spelt flour
85 g (3 oz/½ cup) wholemeal (whole-wheat) spelt flour
80 ml (2½ fl oz/⅓ cup) extra-virgin olive oil

Preheat the oven to 180°C (350°F).

Combine the dry ingredients in a large bowl and mix well. Add 125 ml (4 fl oz/½ cup) water and the oil and mix to form a dough.

Divide the dough in half. Measure two sheets of baking paper the same size as your baking trays, sandwich one half of the dough between the sheets of baking paper and roll out to a 2 mm (⅛ in) thickness. Repeat with the other half of the dough using another two sheets of baking paper.

Remove the top layers of baking paper, and transfer the bottom layers of baking paper, with the dough on top, onto two baking trays.

Sprinkle a little more salt over the top, then put in the oven. Bake for 20–25 minutes, or until the crackers are crisp and slightly golden.

Remove from the oven and leave to cool for 15 minutes. Cut or break the crackers into large shards.

CREAMED CORN (NO CREAM)

——◇——

Corn stock gives this dish a burst of flavour, replacing the need for any butter or cream. This is my number-one choice to eat with roast chicken any day – try Brined roast chicken with chimichurri (page 117). A final drizzle of good-quality extra-virgin olive oil is a must.

SERVES 4-6

6 corn cobs, husks removed
2 teaspoons salt, plus extra to taste
2 tablespoons olive oil or butter
extra-virgin olive oil, for drizzling

Cut the kernels off the corn cobs and set aside.

Make a corn cob stock by combining the corn cobs and salt with 1 litre (34 fl oz/4 cups) water in a saucepan. Place over a medium heat and bring to a simmer, then reduce the heat to low, cover, and keep just below a simmer for at least 1 hour.

Strain the corn stock through a fine-meshed sieve into a clean saucepan over medium heat. Add the corn kernels to the stock and cook for 15 minutes. Remove from the heat.

Allow the stock to cool a little before pouring it into a blender. Blitz until just smooth and creamy. Transfer to a bowl and season to taste with salt. Add the olive oil or butter, and mix well to enrich the corn.

To serve, drizzle with extra-virgin olive oil.

Pictured on page 116.

ROASTED BRUSSELS SPROUTS
◇ WITH ◇
SUNFLOWER SEED PURÉE

With so many nut allergies affecting people these days, sunflower seeds have stolen the limelight and with good reason. They can be used in place of nuts in pestos, salads, cereals, and I've even seen a sunflower seed risotto. This dish is a great side to fish or meat, and the purée would also go well with roasted broccoli or steamed green beans.

SERVES 6-8

1 kg (2 lb 3 oz) brussels sprouts
sea salt and freshly cracked black pepper, for seasoning
3 tablespoons olive oil, plus extra for greasing
juice of ½ lemon
microgreens, for example red radish, to garnish

Sunflower seed purée
500 g (1 lb 2 oz/4 cups) sunflower seeds
2 tablespoons olive oil
100 g (3½ oz) onion, finely diced
1 garlic clove, finely diced
500 ml (17 fl oz/2 cups) chicken or vegetable stock
juice of 1 lemon
125 ml (4 fl oz/½ cup) iced water
sea salt and freshly cracked black pepper, to taste

Preheat the oven to 200°C (400°F).

Spread the brussels sprouts on a lightly oiled baking tray, then season generously with salt and pepper.

Roast in the oven for 40 minutes, or until soft in the centre and caramelised.

To make the sunflower seed purée, put the sunflower seeds in a bowl and cover with cold water. Set aside to soak for 30 minutes, then drain.

Heat the 2 tablespoons of oil in saucepan over low heat. Add the onion and garlic and sauté for 15 minutes, or until soft and golden brown. Add the drained sunflower seeds and cook for a further 10 minutes, stirring constantly.

Add the chicken stock, cover the pan with a lid and simmer gently for 20 minutes, until the seeds are soft enough to blend. Strain and transfer the solids to a food process or blender.

Add the lemon juice and iced water, and blend, in two-second bursts, into a fine purée. Season to taste with salt and pepper.

Pile the brussels sprouts on a platter, drizzle with the remaining oil and the lemon juice and garnish with the microgreens. Serve the purée on the side.

GREENS
—◇ WITH ◇—
CHILLI AND GARLIC

I've been known to eat these braised greens three times in one day: scrambled with eggs for breakfast, in a sandwich with mozzarella for lunch, and as a side to meat or fish for dinner. They can be served at room temperature or reheated, but are best eaten on the day they're made.

SERVES 6–8

2 bunches silverbeet (Swiss chard)
2 bunches cavolo nero
3 tablespoons salt
300 ml (10 fl oz) extra-virgin olive oil
2 garlic cloves, sliced
1 long red chilli, sliced
2 handfuls English spinach
sea salt and freshly cracked black pepper,
   to taste

Remove the silverbeet leaves from the stalks, and cut the stalks into 2.5 cm (1 in) pieces. Do the same with the cavolo nero.

Combine the salt with 4 litres (135 fl oz/16 cups) water in a large heavy-based saucepan and bring to the boil.

Blanch the silverbeet and cavolo nero stalks in the boiling water for 4 minutes. Add the silverbeet and cavolo nero leaves and blanch for a further 30 seconds, until just wilted.

Drain all the blanched greens and set aside.

Heat the oil in a saucepan over medium heat and fry the garlic for 30 seconds, then add the chilli and blanched greens, and fry for 1 minute. Add the spinach and fry for a further minute. Season to taste with salt and pepper.

Pictured on page 116.

CHARGRILLED BROCCOLINI
◇ WITH ◇
GREEN TAHINI

This is perhaps the most versatile side dish you'll ever make. Not only is it super healthy and dairy-free, but it can be served with just about anything. It's great on a grazing table, as a salad or on its own. At Miss Ruben we add roasted almonds to the broccolini before topping it with the chili and garlic oil.

SERVES 8–10

4 bunches broccolini
4 tablespoons olive oil
4 garlic cloves, finely sliced
1 red chilli, halved, seeded and finely sliced
sea salt and freshly cracked black pepper,
    to taste

Green tahini
1 cup Tahini dip (page 31)
15 g (½ oz/½ cup) coriander (cilantro) leaves
10 g (¼ oz/½ cup) mint
10 g (¼ oz/½ cup) flat-leaf (Italian) parsley
sea salt, to taste
lemon juice, to taste

Fill a large saucepan with salted water and bring to the boil. Add the broccolini and blanch for 30 seconds. Drain and pat dry with paper towel.

Heat a chargrill pan or barbecue chargrill plate until hot. Sear the broccolini on each side for 30 seconds, or until slightly charred.

Heat the oil in a frying pan over medium–high heat. Fry the garlic and chilli for 1 minute. Remove the pan from the heat and allow the garlic and chilli to keep cooking in the residual heat.

To make the green tahini, combine the tahini dip and herbs in a food processor or blender, and blend until smooth and creamy. Check the seasoning, and add salt and lemon juice if necessary. If the mixture is too thick, mix in a couple of tablespoons of cold water to loosen.

To serve, spoon the tahini onto a platter, top with the chargrilled broccolini and scatter with the chilli and garlic. Season with salt and pepper to taste.

Pictured on page 136.

SWEET AND
—◇ SOUR ◇—
EGGPLANT CAPONATA

This is a Sicilian dish of eggplant sautéed in a sweet and sour sauce and lots of olive oil.
Feel free to add pine nuts or sultanas, which are also traditional.

SERVES 6-8

125 ml (4 fl oz/½ cup) olive oil, plus extra
  if needed
1 red onion, finely diced
1 garlic clove, finely chopped
1½ red capsicums (bell peppers), diced
4 large eggplants (aubergines), cut into cubes
12 cherry tomatoes, cut in half
2 tablespoons capers in brine, drained
1 teaspoon salt
3 teaspoons caster (superfine) sugar
3 tablespoons red wine vinegar
juice of 1 lemon
2 tablespoons torn basil, to garnish

Heat 85 ml (2¾ fl oz) of the oil in a large saucepan over high heat and add the red onion, garlic and capsicum. Reduce the heat to medium and fry for 25 minutes, or until the onion and capsicums are soft and caramelised.

Meanwhile, heat the remaining oil in a large frying pan over medium–high heat. Working in batches, fry the eggplant for 2 minutes, stirring regularly and adding more oil as needed, until golden brown all over and just cooked. Remove the eggplant from the frying pan and set aside.

Add the tomatoes to the frying pan and fry for 2 minutes, then remove from the heat and set aside.

Add the eggplant and tomatoes to the onion mixture in the saucepan. Add the capers, salt, sugar, red wine vinegar and lemon juice, and cook for 8–10 minutes over low heat.

To serve, transfer to a serving bowl and garnish with the basil.

DESSERTS

CHALLAH BREAD AND BUTTER PUDDING
◇ WITH ◇
POACHED PEARS AND APRICOTS

Despite its name there's no butter in this recipe. Challah – Friday night bread – is rich enough on its own, and paired with home-made egg custard, it's extremely decadent. For best results, prepare the challah and custard the day before. Make sure you serve this warm with lashings of vanilla bean ice cream.

SERVES 8–10

1 challah loaf, about 550 g (1 lb 3 oz)
7 whole eggs
3 egg yolks
60 ml (2 fl oz/¼ cup) sherry
750 ml (25½ fl oz/3 cups) thick (double/heavy) cream
1 teaspoon vanilla paste
1½ teaspoons ground cinnamon
90 g (3 oz/¾ cup) sultanas (golden raisins)
180 g (6½ oz/1 cup) dried apricots
185 g (6½ oz/1 cup) light brown sugar
butter, for greasing
55 g (2 oz/1 cup) coconut flakes, to garnish (optional)
4 tablespoons apricot jam
vanilla bean ice cream, to serve

Poached pears
8 pears, peeled, quartered and seeded
185 g (6½ oz/1 cup) light brown sugar
2 teaspoons ground cinnamon
2 teaspoons lemon juice

Candied oranges
2 oranges
460 g (1 lb/2 cups) caster (superfine) sugar

Tear the challah loaf into pieces, approximately 8 cm (3¼ in) long.

Make a custard by whisking together the eggs, egg yolks, sherry and cream in a large bowl until light and fluffy. Stir in the vanilla paste, cinnamon, sultanas, apricots and sugar.

Mix the challah into the custard, then transfer the mixture to an airtight container with a lid. Refrigerate for at least 6 hours, or overnight. This will allow the bread to soak up the custard.

Preheat the oven to 180°C (350°F).

To make the poached pears, combine all the ingredients in a saucepan with 625 ml (21 fl oz/2½ cups) water. Bring to the boil, removing any foam that rises to the surface. Reduce the heat to a simmer and cook the pears for 15 minutes, until they are soft when pierced with a knife. Cut the pear pieces in half.

To assemble the pudding, lightly grease a 25 cm (10 in) ovenproof dish. Take the challah and custard out of the fridge and give it a mix. Place half the mixture in the dish and lay the pear pieces on top. Spread the rest of the challah and custard mixture over the pears.

Bake in the oven for 1–1½ hours.

>>

>> To check if the pudding is cooked, gently push the centre. No custard should seep out. The top of the pudding should be browned and firm to the touch. Remove from the oven and reduce the oven temperature to 170°C (340°F) if you are using the coconut flakes, otherwise switch off.

While the pudding is cooking, prepare the candied oranges. Cut the oranges horizontally into 4 mm (¼ in) round slices. You should have approximately 28 slices.

Combine the sugar with 750 ml (25½ fl oz/3 cups) water in a saucepan over medium heat. Stir gently for 5 minutes, until the sugar has dissolved. Add the orange slices, bring to the boil, then reduce the heat to low and simmer for 1½ hours. The liquid should have reduced to a syrup consistency. Transfer the orange slices to a wire rack with baking paper underneath to catch any syrup.

Spread the coconut flakes, if using, on a baking tray lined with baking paper, then transfer to the oven and toast for 3–4 minutes, tossing halfway through. Keep an eye on the flakes as they can burn easily.

Pass the apricot jam through a fine-meshed sieve into a small saucepan. Heat gently over low heat for 2–3 minutes. Glaze the pudding with the jam while both are still warm.

To finish the pudding, lay the candied oranges on top and scatter with the toasted coconut flakes, if using. Serve warm with vanilla bean ice cream.

KER D. CHIRICO
CHALLAH

FIG CROSTATA
◇ WITH ◇
ROSEMARY CUSTARD

Figs are believed to have originated in the Middle East and have a strong presence in the Bible, beginning in the Garden of Eden. In late summer and early autumn, take advantage of their sweet flavour and luxurious texture by showcasing them in this rustic crostata. It's best served warm, straight from the oven.

SERVES 6–8

240 g (8½ oz) plain (all-purpose) flour, plus extra for dusting
80 g (2¾ oz/⅓ cup) caster (superfine) sugar
pinch of salt
120 g (4½ oz) cold butter, cubed
2 egg yolks
90 g (3 oz/¾ cup) semolina
8 fresh figs, sliced in half lengthways
1 egg, beaten, for glazing
icing (confectioners') sugar, for dusting (optional)

Rosemary custard
750 ml (25½ fl oz/3 cups) milk
2 rosemary sprigs
3 egg yolks
70 g (2½ oz) caster (superfine) sugar
2 tablespoons cornflour (cornstarch)

Place the flour, sugar, salt and butter in a food processor and pulse until the mixture resembles coarse crumbs. Add the egg yolks and 2 tablespoons cold water, and blitz again until the dough comes together.

Tip the dough out onto a floured surface and shape into a ball then flatten slightly. Wrap in plastic wrap and rest in the refrigerator for 30 minutes.

Preheat the oven to 200°C (400°F).

Roll out the dough into a large circle with a diameter of 30 cm (12 in). Line a baking tray with baking paper and sprinkle one-third of the semolina on top. Place the dough on top of the semolina and sprinkle the remaining semolina on top of the dough.

Arrange the figs on top of the pastry in an inner circle with a diameter of about 20 cm (8 in). You should be left with a 10 cm (4 in) ring of pastry around the fruit. Fold up the edges of the pastry over the fruit. Glaze the pastry flap with the beaten egg and place in the oven to bake for 50 minutes.

While the crostata is baking, make the rosemary custard. Pour the milk into a large saucepan over medium–low heat, add the rosemary sprigs and warm through to infuse for 5–10 minutes.

In a bowl, vigorously whisk the egg yolks with the sugar and cornflour to form a paste.

When the milk is warm, remove the rosemary and pour 250 ml (8½ fl oz/1 cup) of the warm milk into the egg mixture. Gently combine, then pour the mixture back into the saucepan with remaining milk. Stir continuously over low heat until the custard thickens.

Remove the crostata from the oven. Dust with icing sugar, if using, and serve with the rosemary custard on the side.

ROASTED PEACH, PECAN
◇ AND ◇
SPELT CRUMBLE WITH LEMON CURD

Serve this during the summer months when peaches are at their best. It goes really well with the tangy, sweet flavour of the lemon curd.

SERVES 10–12

2 kg (4 lb 6 oz) peaches, stones removed and cut into 2 cm (¾ in) wedges
165 g (6 oz) light muscovado sugar
2 tablespoons plain (all-purpose) flour
juice of ½ lemon
½ teaspoon ground cinnamon
½ teaspoon natural vanilla extract
vanilla bean ice cream or custard, to serve

Crumble topping
150 g (5½ oz) butter, softened
225 g (8 oz) spelt flour
150 g (5½ oz) light muscovado sugar
75 g (2¾ oz) oats
1½ teaspoons ground cinnamon
90 g (3 oz) pecans, chopped in half

Lemon curd
250 g (9 oz) caster (superfine) sugar
6 eggs
juice of 7 lemons
250 g (9 oz) butter, softened

Preheat the oven to 170°C (340°F).

Put the peaches and sugar in a bowl and mix well to combine. Leave to stand for 30 minutes.

Add the flour, lemon juice, cinnamon and vanilla to the sugared peaches, then transfer the mixture to a 25 cm (10 in) ovenproof dish.

Cover the dish with foil and cook in the oven for about 30 minutes, until the peaches are soft.

While the peaches are cooking, prepare the crumble topping. Put the softened butter in a mixing bowl, then add all the dry ingredients and rub together with your fingers to make a crumb.

Remove the peaches from the oven and drain off the excess juice. Top with the crumble mixture and return to the oven. Bake, uncovered, for 30–40 minutes, until the crumble is lightly coloured on top.

To make the lemon curd, combine the sugar, eggs and lemon juice in a heavy-based saucepan. Place the pan over low heat and whisk constantly, for 5–7 minutes, until the curd has thickened.

Remove from the heat and strain through a fine-meshed sieve into a bowl. While the mixture is still hot, whisk in the softened butter with a balloon whisk until well combined.

Serve the peach crumble warm with the lemon curd and ice cream or custard.

BRANDIED ORANGES

◇

This recipe first appeared in *Cooking from the Heart*, a book my friends Hayley Smorgon and Gaye Weeden compiled with recipes and stories of Jewish cooks in Melbourne. It was actually part of a menu my mum submitted for that book, and it is still one of my favourite dishes to end a meal with. The oranges are really refreshing and best served chilled, and they make a great alternative to the blood plum compote with the Flourless chocolate torte (page 197). If you can, prepare the dish the day before so the oranges can soak up all the syrupy goodness.

SERVES 8–10

8 oranges
345 g (12 oz/1½ cups) caster (superfine) sugar
60 ml (2 fl oz/¼ cup) brandy
2 cinnamon sticks
2 star anise

Peel the oranges, ensuring you remove all the bitter white pith. Slice the oranges crossways into thin slices or cut them into segments. Place in a serving bowl.

Combine the sugar and 500 ml (17 fl oz/2 cups) water in a saucepan and set over low heat. Stir until the sugar dissolves, about 5 minutes. Add the brandy, increase the heat to high and boil the mixture for 5–10 minutes, then remove from the heat.

Add the cinnamon sticks and star anise, then pour the syrup over the oranges. Refrigerate until cool, or overnight.

ROASTED RHUBARB
—◇— WITH —◇—
ORANGE AND VANILLA

I love ending a meal with fruit, and once you've mastered roasting rhubarb, you'll do it time and time again. The key to getting it soft but not mushy is in the amount of liquid you add and keeping an eye on it while it's cooking. Its uses are endless: as a crumble base, in a butter cake, with granola or together with a big bowl of strawberries and your favourite ice cream or yoghurt.

SERVES 6-8

2 bunches rhubarb, leaves removed, cut into 5 cm (2 in) lengths
200 g (7 oz) light brown sugar
2 vanilla beans
2 cinnamon sticks
1 orange
vanilla bean ice cream or yoghurt, to serve

Preheat the oven to 180°C (350°F).

Place the rhubarb in an ovenproof dish, then rub all over with the sugar.

Split the vanilla beans lengthways and scrape out the seeds. Add the vanilla beans and seeds and cinnamon sticks to the dish with the rhubarb.

Peel the orange, adding the peel to the dish. Halve, then squeeze the orange juice over the rhubarb and add the squeezed halves to the dish.

Pour in 80 ml (2½ fl oz/⅓ cup) water, then cover with foil.

Roast the rhubarb in the oven for 30 minutes, checking the liquid halfway through – it should cover half of the rhubarb (otherwise, add extra water). Once cooked, the rhubarb should still be reasonably firm and not soggy.

Remove from the oven, still covered, and leave to cool.

Serve with ice cream or yoghurt.

ROASTED QUINCES
◇ WITH ◇
BLUEBERRY LABNE

Quinces are an ancient fruit native to Turkey and Southeast Asia. While too hard and tart to be eaten raw, they transform when cooked into stunning crimson jewels. The quinces need to be roasted the day before, and the labne also needs to drain overnight. Don't be alarmed by the amount of sugar – it's needed for the quinces to change colour, and the blueberry labne strikes a nice balance.

SERVES 8–10

10 quinces
1 lemon, sliced
800 g (1 lb 12 oz) caster (superfine) sugar
2 cinnamon sticks
2 vanilla beans

Labne
500 ml (17 fl oz/2 cups) sheep's milk yoghurt

Blueberry compote
310 g (11 oz/2 cups) blueberries, frozen or fresh
460 g (1 lb /2 cups) caster (superfine) sugar
¼ cup lemon juice

Preheat the oven to 110°C (230°F).

Peel the quinces, placing them in a bowl of water with the lemon slices as you go. This will prevent the quinces from discolouring. Reserve the quince peel.

Cut the quinces in half and remove and discard the cores and seeds.

Slice the vanilla beans lengthways and scrape out the seeds.

Combine the sugar, 2 litres (68 fl oz/8 cups) water, the vanilla beans and seeds, cinnamon sticks, and quince peel in a saucepan over medium heat. Bring to a simmer and stir until the sugar has dissolved.

Place the quinces in a deep baking tray and pour over the sugar liquid. Add a little more water if necessary to ensure the quinces are completely covered.

Cover the tray with foil and roast in the oven for 5–6 hours. Once cooked, turn off the oven and let the quinces cool in the oven overnight.

To make the labne, place the yoghurt in a fine-meshed sieve lined with muslin (cheesecloth). Place the sieve over a bowl or container, tie the muslin over the yoghurt and leave to drain overnight in the refrigerator.

The next day, make the blueberry compote by combining the ingredients in a saucepan. Bring to the boil, then reduce the heat to medium and stir for 8–10 minutes, until the sugar has dissolved. Remove from the heat and leave to cool completely.

When you're ready to serve, place the labne in a serving bowl and top with blobs of blueberry compote. Gently swirl together to create a ripple effect.

Serve the quinces cold with a dollop of blueberry labne.

TAHINI DATE CHEWS

◇

This recipe was given to me by Seed + Mill, a sesame concept store based in New York's Chelsea Market. Started by three women from three corners of the globe – including one Sydneysider – it's the first of its kind in the USA and I love what they do. These are gluten-free and vegan: a great healthy afternoon pick-me-up.

MAKES 12

10 medjool dates, pitted
2 tablespoons maple syrup
2 tablespoons tahini
1 tablespoon coconut oil
2 teaspoons natural vanilla extract
175 g (6 oz/1 cup) dairy-free dark chocolate couverture buds or small buttons
pink Himalayan sea salt, to sprinkle

Combine the dates, maple syrup, tahini, coconut oil and vanilla extract in a food processor, and pulse to form a smooth paste.

Tip the mixture out onto a sheet of plastic wrap, roll up tightly and refrigerate for 30–40 minutes, until firm.

Once hard, slice the date mixture into small bite-sized pieces.

Melt the chocolate in a double boiler and dip the date pieces into the chocolate one by one. Transfer the chews to a baking tray lined with baking paper. Before the chocolate sets, sprinkle each chew with a little pink salt.

Allow the chocolate to cool and harden before eating.

FLOURLESS CHOCOLATE TORTE
◇ WITH ◇
BLOOD PLUM COMPOTE

You wouldn't know that this dessert is both gluten-free and dairy-free – it looks and tastes ridiculously good, and is a great recipe for Pesach. Team with blood plums in summer or Roasted quinces (page 193) when temperatures drop. If you eat dairy, a scoop of chocolate ice cream pushes it right over the top.

SERVES 8–10

olive oil spray, for greasing
6 eggs
100 g (3½ oz) caster (superfine) sugar
100 g (3½ oz) light brown sugar
300 g (10½ oz) dairy-free dark chocolate couverture, roughly chopped
2 tablespoons good-quality ground coffee
2 tablespoons Dutch (unsweetened) cocoa powder, to serve

Blood plum compote
1 kg (2 lb 3 oz) blood plums, quartered, stones removed, and flesh roughly chopped
juice of 2 oranges
6 long strips of orange zest, approximately 2 cm (¾ in) thick
85 g (3 oz) caster (superfine) sugar
1 teaspoon vanilla paste

Preheat the oven to 180°C (350°F). Grease a 25 cm (10 in) round cake tin with olive oil spray and line it with baking paper.

In the bowl of a stand mixer, whisk the eggs and sugars for about 5 minutes, or until light and creamy.

Melt the chocolate in a double boiler and leave to cool to room temperature, then slowly pour the melted chocolate into the egg mixture, whisking continuously. Gently fold in the coffee powder.

Pour the batter into the prepared tin and place in the oven. Bake for 30 minutes, until the torte has risen and feels slightly firm. Remove from the oven and leave to cool completely in the tin.

While the torte is baking, make the blood plum compote. Combine the plums, orange juice and zest and sugar in a large saucepan and bring to the boil, stirring occasionally.

Reduce the heat to medium and simmer, stirring from time to time, for about 15 minutes, then mix in the vanilla paste and remove from the heat. The fruit should be softened but still holding its shape.

To serve, turn the torte out of its tin and transfer to a platter. Dust generously with cocoa powder and serve with the blood plum compote.

HALVA CHEESECAKE

◇

Halva fans will be left dreaming about this cake with its smooth, rich sesame-flavoured filling. I like to use plain halva in the body of the cake but top it with chunks of the chocolate-flavoured stuff just to make it even more irresistible. It's a perfect cake to make for Shavout, when it's traditional to eat milk products.

SERVES 10–12

Crust
200 g (7 oz) Marie biscuits or other sweet plain biscuits
6 tablespoons butter, melted, plus extra for greasing

Filling
600 g (1 lb 5 oz) plain halva, crushed
185 ml (6 fl oz/¾ cup) thick (double/heavy) cream
1.5 kg (3 lb 5 oz) quark
6 eggs
120 g (4½ oz) chocolate halva, crumbled, to serve

Grease a 25 cm (10 in) springform cake tin and line it with baking paper.

To make the crust, add the biscuits to a food processor and blitz to a fine crumb. Transfer to a mixing bowl.

Add the melted butter and mix until thoroughly combined. Pour the mixture into the cake tin and press down firmly to form a crust. Refrigerate while you make the filling.

Preheat the oven to 160°C (320°F).

To make the filling, combine the plain halva and cream in a frying pan over low heat. Cook, stirring gently, until the halva has completely dissolved. Remove from the heat and leave to cool.

Put the quark in a clean food processor. Add the eggs, one at a time, blending well after each is added. Add the halva mixture and stir to combine.

Pour the filling over the crust and bake in the oven for 1 hour and 20 minutes.

Leave the cake to cool completely before decorating with crumbled chocolate halva to serve.

MIDDLE EASTERN FRUIT SALAD
◇ WITH ◇
CASHEW CREAM

There was always a bowl of stewed dried fruits, or 'compote' as we called it, in my grandparents' fridge and it appeared at the end of every meal. This version combines dried apricots with fresh peaches, figs, citrus fruits and grapes to make it healthier and more sophisticated. Persimmons add an exotic touch but only have a limited season in Australia; replace with mango or nectarine when unavailable. The cashew cream is a delicious alternative to dairy – it's a little bit earthy and not too sweet.

SERVES 6-8

200 g (7 oz) dried apricots
seeds of 1 vanilla bean
1 cinnamon stick
1 star anise
500 ml (17 fl oz/2 cups) apple juice
175 g (6 oz/½ cup) honey
3 yellow peaches, halved, stones removed
150 g (5½ oz) red grapes, cut in half
2 blood oranges or small pink grapefruits, segmented
1 persimmon, sliced
3 black figs, sliced
mint sprigs, to garnish

Cashew cream
155 g (5½ oz/1 cup) raw cashews, soaked in cold water for a minimum of 3 hours
1 tablespoon honey
seeds of 1 pomegranate, to garnish

Combine the apricots, vanilla seeds, cinnamon stick, star anise, apple juice and honey in a saucepan. Place over high heat and bring to the boil, then reduce the heat to medium–low and simmer for 12 minutes, until the apricots are soft and the liquid is slightly reduced. Remove the cinnamon stick and star anise, and set aside.

Cut each peach half into roughly six segments. Place the peaches and grapes in a mixing bowl. Pour in the apricot mixture, stir to combine, and leave to cool completely.

To make the cashew cream, drain the cashews, retaining the soaking water. Place the cashews in a high-speed blender with 190 ml (6½ fl oz) of the soaking water. Blend until you have a smooth cream, about 2 minutes. Stir in the honey.

When the grapes and peaches are cool, add the orange segments and sliced persimmon and spoon into a serving bowl. Scatter the sliced figs over the top and garnish with mint sprigs.

Top the cashew cream with pomegranate seeds and serve with the fruit salad.

BLINTZES
—◇ WITH ◇—
ZUCCOTTO FILLING AND SOUR CHERRY SAUCE

Blintzes get an Italian makeover here; the zuccotto filling with amaretto liquor, dark chocolate and dried fruit is totally decadent. The sour cherry sauce can also be served with our Rolled roast turkey breast (page 124). Try and find dried sour cherries from the Middle East; they are superior to most others I've tried.

MAKES 15–20

Zuccotto filling
100 g (3½ oz) dried sour cherries
100 g (3½ oz) dried pears
250 ml (8½ fl oz/1 cup) amaretto
150 g (5½ oz/1 cup) dark chocolate couverture, broken into pieces
155 g (5½ oz/1 cup) toasted almonds
400 g (14 oz) full-cream ricotta
100 g (3½ oz) quark
2 tablespoons caster (superfine) sugar

Crêpe batter
3 eggs
225 g (8 oz/1½ cups) plain (all-purpose) flour
pinch of salt
½ teaspoon baking powder
olive oil spray, for greasing

Sour cherry sauce
125 ml (4 fl oz/½ cup) sour cherry juice or water
55 g (2 oz/¼ cup) sugar, 85 g (3 oz) if using water instead of cherry juice
2 teaspoons cornflour (cornstarch)
400 g (14 oz/2 cups) pitted sour cherries from a jar

To make the zuccotto filling, soak the dried cherries and pears in the amaretto for 3–4 hours. Drain and finely dice.

Place the chocolate in the freezer for 30 minutes, then combine with the almonds in a food processor. Blitz for approximately 50 seconds, until you have a rough crumb.

Combine the ricotta, quark, sugar, dried fruit, chocolate and nuts in a bowl and mix well.

Preheat the oven to 180°C (350°F).

To make the crêpe batter, beat the eggs with 750 ml (25½ fl oz/3 cups) water in a large bowl. Sift in the flour, salt and baking powder, and beat until smooth. Leave the batter to rest for 10 minutes.

Heat a non-stick crêpe pan or 20 cm (8 in) frying pan over low heat and grease lightly with olive oil spray. Pour enough batter into the pan to thinly coat the base, swirling the pan so the batter spreads to the edge. Cook the crêpe on one side only over low heat for 2–3 minutes, until it is lightly coloured and comes away from the side of the pan. Put aside on a plate, and repeat with the remaining mixture.

Place 50–80 g (1¾–2¾ oz) of the ricotta mixture in the centre of each crêpe. Fold over the sides, then roll up and rest on the seam. Transfer to a greased ovenproof dish and cover with foil. Heat in the oven for 10 minutes.

To make the sour cherry sauce, pour the juice or water into a saucepan. Add the sugar and cornflour, and whisk until smooth. Bring to a boil over medium heat and cook until slightly thickened, about 1 minute. Stir the cherries through, then let the sauce cool a little.

Pour the sauce over the crêpes to serve.

CARROT CAKE
—◇ WITH ◇—
WHIPPED COCONUT ICING

This cake even sounds healthy: carrots, pineapple, pistachios, wholemeal flour and olive oil topped with a whipped coconut yoghurt. It's super moist and more-ish.

SERVES 12

6 eggs
500 ml (17 fl oz/2 cups) light olive oil, plus extra for greasing
3 carrots, grated
440 g (15½ oz) tinned crushed pineapples, drained
150 g (5½ oz/1 cup) pistachios, chopped
2 teaspoons ground cinnamon
1 teaspoon ground nutmeg
450 g (1 lb/3 cups) plain wholemeal (whole-wheat) flour
440 g (15½ oz/2 cups) caster (superfine) sugar
3 tablespoons baking powder
1 teaspoon bicarbonate of soda (baking soda)
30 g (1 oz) coconut flakes, to garnish

Whipped coconut icing
560 ml (19 fl oz/2¼ cups) dairy-free plain coconut yoghurt (such as Coyo)
55 g (2 oz) icing (confectioners') sugar

Preheat the oven to 180°C (350°F).

Lightly grease a 25 cm (10 in) springform cake tin with oil and line with baking paper.

Lightly whisk together the eggs and olive oil in a large bowl. Add the remaining ingredients, except the coconut flakes, and stir until well combined.

Pour the mixture into the prepared cake tin and bake for 45 minutes to 1 hour, until a skewer inserted in the centre comes out clean.

While the cake is baking, prepare the icing. Place the coconut yoghurt and icing sugar in the bowl of a stand mixture fitted with the whisk attachment. Whisk for 2 minutes, or until stiff peaks form.

Remove the cake from the oven and leave to cool in the tin, and reduce the oven temperature to 170°C (390°F).

Spread the coconut flakes on a baking tray lined with baking paper, then transfer to the oven and toast for 3–4 minutes, tossing halfway through. Keep an eye on the flakes as they can burn easily.

To serve, turn the cake out onto a platter and spread the coconut icing on top. Garnish with toasted coconut flakes.

CHOCOLATE SWIRL PAVLOVA
◇ WITH ◇
ROSEWATER CREAM, TURKISH DELIGHT AND STRAWBERRIES

Bright, festive and bountiful, this chocolate swirl pavlova with its Middle Eastern flavours is a real show stopper. In winter we flavour the cream with orange blossom and top the pav with roasted pears and pistachios.

SERVES 10–12

9 egg whites
690 g (1½ lb/3 cups) caster (superfine) sugar
1½ teaspoons cornflour (cornstarch), sifted
2 tablespoons Dutch (unsweetened) cocoa powder
¾ teaspoon white vinegar
500 ml (17 fl oz/2 cups) thick (double/heavy) cream
1 tablespoon rosewater
750 g (1 lb 11 oz) strawberries, cut into thick slices and halves
150 g (5½ oz) Turkish delight, cut into 2 cm (¾ in) pieces
rose petals, to garnish (optional)

Preheat the oven to 180°C (350°F). Cut out a 30 cm (12 in) circle of baking paper and place it in the middle of a baking tray.

To make the pavlova, place the egg whites in the bowl of a stand mixer and beat on high speed until stiff peaks form. While the machine is still running, gradually add the sugar in four batches, beating well between each addition until the sugar has dissolved. This will take 10–15 minutes.

Fold in the cornflour, half the cocoa powder and the vinegar until well combined. Gently stir through the remaining cocoa powder to create a swirl effect.

Using a large spoon, scoop the meringue onto the baking paper circle until the baking paper is covered. Smooth the top of the meringue, making a slight dip in the centre.

Place the meringue in the oven and immediately reduce the temperature to 120°C (240°F). Bake for 2 hours, until crisp and dry. Turn the oven off and leave the meringue inside, with the door slightly ajar, to cool completely.

Whip the cream and rosewater together until thick.

Top the meringue base with the rosewater cream and decorate with the Turkish delight, strawberries and rose petals, if using.

APPLE
—◇ AND ◇—
POPPY SEED CAKE

This is a recipe from my late grandmother, Saba Eckhaus – her poppy seed cake was legendary, and when my mum went into catering it would appear on many afternoon tea tables. The grated apple and oil makes it really light. I've made the icing dairy-free so it can be served after a meat meal, but make a more decadent chocolate ganache using cream if you're serving it after fish.

SERVES 14

olive oil spray, for greasing
9 eggs, separated
345 g (12 oz/1½ cups) caster (superfine) sugar
¾ teaspoon natural vanilla extract
3 green apples, peeled, cored and grated
¾ teaspoon baking powder
35 g (1¼ oz/¼ cup) self-raising flour
400 g (14 oz) poppy seeds

Dairy-free chocolate ganache
500 g (1 lb 2 oz) dairy-free dark chocolate
   couverture, broken into pieces
350 ml (12 fl oz) almond or soy milk
1 tablespoon liquid glucose

Preheat the oven to 180°C (350°F). Grease a 25 cm (10 in) springform cake tin and line it with baking paper.

Using an electric mixer, beat the egg yolks and sugar in a large mixing bowl until fluffy and pale in colour. Add the vanilla, stirring to mix well, then add the remaining ingredients.

In another large bowl, beat the egg whites using a clean electric mixer until stiff peaks form. Gently fold into the batter using a metal spoon.

Pour the mixture into the pre-prepared tin, cover with foil, and bake in the oven for 45 minutes.

Remove the foil and bake for another 45 minutes.

Remove and cool the cake in the tin for 30 minutes before turning it out of the tin onto a wire rack to cool completely.

While the cake is cooling, make the ganache. Melt the chocolate in a double boiler. Heat the milk in a saucepan over medium heat until just below boiling point. Remove from the heat and pour the milk over the chocolate. Add the glucose and stir gently until you have a smooth, shiny ganache.

Spread the ganache over the cake and cut into slices to serve.

LEMON CHIFFON CAKE
◇ WITH ◇
PASSIONFRUIT ICING

This is my son Cooper's favourite cake and you'll usually find a version sitting on our kitchen bench. Light and fluffy, a chiffon cake gets it height from whipping air into the egg whites. You'll need an angel cake tin – just don't be tempted to oil it, because the cake will fall out.

SERVES 12

8 eggs, separated
345 g (12 oz/1½ cups) caster (superfine) sugar
190 ml (6½ fl oz) grapeseed oil
190 ml (6½ fl oz) fresh lemon juice
zest of ½ lemon
225 g (8 oz/1½ cups) self-raising flour, sifted

Passionfruit icing
125 g (4½ oz/1 cup) icing (confectioners') sugar
3 tablespoons passionfruit pulp

Preheat the oven to 180°C (350°F).

Place the egg whites in a large mixing bowl and whisk with an electric mixer until soft peaks form. Slowly add 115 g (4 oz/½ cup) of the sugar and continue whisking until the egg whites are stiff, but not too dry.

In a separate bowl, beat the egg yolks and the remaining sugar with an electric mixer until light and fluffy. Add the oil and continue beating for a couple of minutes, until well combined. Add the lemon juice and lemon zest, and mix well.

Gradually add the flour to the egg yolk mixture, beating well in between each addition to make sure the flour is fully incorporated. Gently fold in the egg whites using a metal spoon.

Pour the mixture into an angel cake tin and bake for 1 hour, or until a skewer inserted in the centre comes out clean.

Remove the cake from the oven and immediately invert onto a glass bottle, such as a wine bottle, with the neck sitting in the tin's central funnel. Leave to cool completely.

To make the icing, sift the icing sugar into a bowl, add the passionfruit pulp, and whisk until combined. The icing should have the consistency of thick cream.

Once the cake is cool, run a knife around the outside of the cake and the central funnel. Lift the base out of the tin, then use a knife to ease the cake off the base.

Pour the icing in a thin stream over the cake, and let it spread as it falls.

ORANGE
—◇ AND ◇—
CINNAMON KUGELHOPF

These days most of us associate chocolate with a kugelhopf. Here is another version of this famous sweet yeasted bread, traditionally baked in a high fluted mould and popular in Alsace, France. Almost panettone-like in texture, it's plumped up with currants, orange peel and almonds, and can be eaten for afternoon tea or toasted for breakfast served with a good coffee.

SERVES 10–12

250 ml (8½ fl oz/1 cup) warm milk
2 tablespoons honey
1 tablespoon dried yeast
450 g (1 lb oz/3 cups) plain (all-purpose) flour
180 g (6½ oz) butter, slightly softened, plus extra for greasing
110 g (4 oz/½ cup) caster (superfine) sugar
4 eggs, separated
½ teaspoon natural vanilla extract
1 teaspoon ground cinnamon
½ teaspoon salt
150 g (5½ oz/1 cup) currants
zest of 1 orange
60 g (2 oz/½ cup) slivered almonds
1½ tablespoons icing (confectioners') sugar, for dusting (optional)

Combine the milk and honey in a bowl. Sprinkle the yeast over the top and leave for 10 minutes to bloom.

Add 150 g (5½ oz/1 cup) of the flour to the yeast mixture and stir to combine. Cover and set the starter aside for 30 minutes.

In the bowl of a stand mixer fitted with the paddle attachment, cream the butter and sugar until smooth and fluffy. Add the starter and mix again until combined.

Scrape down the sides of the bowl and, with the mixer still running, add the egg yolks one at a time. Add the vanilla, cinnamon, salt, currants, orange zest and another 300 g (10½ oz/2 cups) of the flour. Mix well.

In another bowl, using a clean electric mixer, beat the egg whites to soft peaks, then fold into the cake mixture using a metal spoon.

Preheat the oven to 180°C (350°F).

Grease the kugelhopf mould generously with butter and sprinkle the almonds on the sides and bottom.

Pour the mixture into the mould, making sure it is evenly distributed. Cover loosely with plastic wrap and set aside for 45 minutes to 1 hour, or until the mixture has risen three-quarters of the way up the side of the tin.

Bake in the oven for 30 minutes, then check the cake. If the exposed cake is browning too quickly, place a piece of foil loosely on top. Bake for another 20–30 minutes, until a skewer inserted in the middle of the cake comes out clean.

Remove the cake from the oven and invert it onto a wire rack to cool completely.

Dust with icing sugar and serve.

SICILIAN APPLE CAKE

—◇—

This cake, full of apples, pine nuts and sultanas, also has the Mediterranean flavours of cinnamon, lemon and vanilla. It's best eaten on the day it's made and should have an almost custard-like texture between the layers of goodness.

SERVES 10–12

75 g (2¾ oz) walnuts
1.5 kg (3 lb 5 oz) granny smith apples, peeled, cored, quartered and sliced
zest and juice of 1 lemon
155 g (5½ oz/1 cup) pine nuts
5 eggs
3 teaspoons vanilla paste
385 g (13½ oz) caster (superfine) sugar, plus extra for sprinkling
160 g (5½ oz) butter, melted, plus extra for greasing
225 g (8 oz) plain (all-purpose) flour
3 tablespoons baking powder
150 ml (5 fl oz) milk
180 g (6½ oz/1½ cups) sultanas (golden raisins)
1½ teaspoons ground cinnamon
1½ tablespoons icing (confectioners') sugar, for dusting

Preheat the oven to 170°C (340°F).

Place the walnuts in a food processor and pulse, in two-second bursts, until evenly ground.

Grease a 25 cm (10 in) cake tin generously with butter, then sprinkle the base and sides with the ground walnuts and set aside.

In a bowl, toss the apple slices with the lemon zest and juice and set aside.

Heat a small frying pan over medium heat and toast the pine nuts, tossing, until lightly brown. Leave to cool.

Combine the eggs, vanilla paste and sugar in the bowl of a stand mixer and whisk together until pale and creamy. Add the melted butter, flour, baking powder and milk, and mix thoroughly.

Pour one-third of the cake batter into the prepared tin, then top with one-third of the apple slices, pine nuts and sultanas.

Repeat with the remaining ingredients, finishing with a layer of apples. Sprinkle the cinnamon and some sugar over the top.

Cover with foil and bake for 45 minutes, then remove the foil and bake for another 45 minutes, or until the top is golden and firm to touch. Remove from the oven and leave to cool in the tin for 20 minutes.

Turn the cake onto a platter and dust with icing sugar before serving.

NEW YEAR HONEY CAKE

—◇—

This honey cake is reminiscent of the one Mebourne's Baker D. Chirico sell at their gorgeous St Kilda store for Rosh Hashanah. They kindly helped me with this recipe to make it work for domestic cooks. A kick of whisky, orange juice and the spices set it apart from any other honey cake I've tried. This recipe makes enough batter to fill two 23 cm (9 in) square or round cake tins, and either one 23–25 cm (9–10 in) ring (bundt) tin or one 23 × 33 cm (9 × 13 in) sheet cake tin. Enjoy with a cup of tea or coffee.

MAKES 1–2

olive oil spray, for greasing
525 g (1 lb 3 oz/3½ cups) plain (all-purpose) flour
1 teaspoon baking powder
1 teaspoon bicarbonate of soda (baking soda)
½ teaspoon salt
1⅓ tablespoons ground cinnamon
½ teaspoon ground cloves
½ teaspoon ground allspice
250 ml (8½ fl oz/1 cup) vegetable oil
350 g (12½ oz/1 cup) honey
345 g (12 oz/1½ cups) caster (superfine) sugar
95 g (3¼ oz/½ cup) light brown sugar
3 large eggs
1 teaspoon natural vanilla extract
250 ml (8½ fl oz/1 cup) warm coffee or strong tea
125 ml (4 fl oz/½ cup) fresh orange juice
60 ml (2 fl oz/¼ cup) whisky
60 g (2 oz/½ cup) slivered or flaked almonds (optional)

Preheat the oven to 180°C (350°F). Generously grease the tin(s) with olive oil spray.

In a large bowl, combine the flour, baking powder, bicarbonate of soda, salt and ground spices. Make a well in the centre and add the oil, honey, sugars, eggs, vanilla, coffee or tea, orange juice and whisky.

Using a strong whisk or an electric mixer on slow speed, whisk the ingredients together to make a thick, well-blended batter, making sure nothing is stuck to the bottom of the bowl.

Spoon the batter into the prepared cake tin(s) and sprinkle the top of the cakes with the almonds, if using.

Stack two baking trays on top of one another, then place the cake tin(s) on top. This will ensure the cakes bake evenly.

Bake until the cakes spring back when touched gently in the centre. For ring (bundt) cakes, this will take 60–75 minutes; for round or square cakes, it will take 45–55 minutes; for sheet cakes, it will take 40–45 minutes.

Allow the cakes to stand for 15 minutes before removing from the tins.

MARBLE CAKE

—◇—

This is a foolproof cake guaranteed to please the whole family. Use the best-quality cocoa you can find, because it really does makes a difference. I've made this with almond milk so it's dairy-free, but you can use full-cream milk in its place. We make our own almond milk at Miss Ruben – it's easy and well worth the effort – but if using a store-bought variety make sure it's fresh, not from a carton.

SERVES 10–12

olive oil spray, for greasing
450 g (1 lb/3 cups) plain (all-purpose) flour, plus extra for dusting
60 g (2 oz/½ cup) Dutch (unsweetened) cocoa powder
500 g (1 lb 2 oz) caster (superfine) sugar
2 teaspoons baking powder
250 ml (8½ fl oz/1 cup) extra-virgin olive oil
1 teaspoon natural vanilla extract
5 cold eggs
fresh raspberries, to serve

Home-made almond milk
155 g (5½ oz/1 cup) almonds, soaked overnight in cold water
dash of natural vanilla extract
1 medjool date, stone removed

To make the almond milk, drain and rinse the almonds. Combine them with the vanilla, date and 750 ml (25½ fl oz/3 cups) water in a blender. Blitz until smooth, then strain through a nut milk bag or fine-meshed sieve lined with muslin (cheesecloth). Refrigerate until ready to use. The nut milk will keep for 4–5 days, refrigerated in an airtight container.

Preheat the oven to 175°C (350°F). Grease a 23 × 13 × 7 cm (9 × 5 × 3 in) loaf tin with the oil spray and dust with flour.

In a large bowl, whisk together the cocoa powder, 100 g (3½ oz/½ cup) of the sugar and 80 ml (2½ fl oz/⅓ cup) water until well blended. Set aside.

In another bowl, combine the flour and baking powder.

In the bowl of a stand mixer fitted with the whisk attachment, beat 400 g (14 oz/2 cups) of the sugar, the oil and vanilla until well combined. Add the eggs, one at a time, beating after each addition. Continue beating for another 3–5 minutes, until the mixture is thick and pale.

Stop the mixer and add one-third of the flour mixture. Beat on low speed until just blended. Stop the mixer again and add 125 ml (4 fl oz/½ cup) of the almond milk. Beat until just blended. Repeat with another one-third of the flour, another 125 ml of the almond milk, and then the remaining flour, beating the mixture after each addition.

Add three cups of the batter to the cocoa mixture and mix well. Pour one-third of the plain batter into the prepared tin and top with one third of the chocolate batter. Continue adding the batter in layers until both mixtures are used.

Bake for 1 hour, or until a skewer inserted in the middle of the cake comes out clean.

Leave the cake to cool in the tin, then turn it out onto a platter. Serve with fresh raspberries.

SALTED CHOC CHIP TAHINI COOKIES

———◇———

This recipe is also from Seed + Mill, the sesame concept store in New York. We couldn't get enough of these giant cookies, so we've added them to the counter at Miss Ruben.

MAKES 12

115 g (4 oz) unsalted butter
110 g (4 oz) tahini
230 g (8 oz/1 cup) caster (superfine) sugar
1 egg
1 egg yolk
1 teaspoon natural vanilla extract
150 g (5½ oz/1 cup) plain (all-purpose) flour
½ teaspoon bicarbonate of soda (baking soda)
½ teaspoon baking powder
½ teaspoon salt
305 g (11 oz/1¾ cup) dairy-free dark chocolate couverture buds or small buttons
115 g (4 oz/¾ cup) sesame seeds
pinch of pink Himalayan sea salt

Using an electric mixer, cream the butter, tahini and sugar in a bowl until light and fluffy.

Add the egg, egg yolk and vanilla and beat for 5 minutes.

Sift the flour, bicarbonate of soda, baking powder and salt into a large mixing bowl and combine with the tahini mixture. Add the chocolate buds and stir.

Line two baking trays with baking paper. Shape the cookie dough into 70 g (2½ oz) balls and roll each ball in the sesame seeds before placing on the trays. Gently flatten them to about 1 cm (½ in) thick. Space them 3 cm (1¼ in) apart, because they do spread. Refrigerate for 1 hour before baking.

Preheat the oven to 190°C (375°F).

Bake the cookies for approximately 15 minutes, or until golden brown. Be careful not to overcook them, because they are better when they're a bit gooey on the inside.

While the cookies are still warm, sprinkle them with pink salt and serve.

NUTELLA COOKIES

—◇—

The giant jar of these cookies at Miss Ruben is only ever half full because we can't make them fast enough.

MAKES 25

150 g (5½ oz) butter, softened
150 g (5½ oz) light brown sugar
145 g (5 oz/⅔ cup) caster (superfine) sugar
2 large eggs
125 g (4½ oz) dark chocolate couverture buds
 or small buttons
75 g (2¾ oz) milk chocolate couverture buds
 or small buttons
300 g (10½ oz/2 cups) plain (all-purpose) flour
50 g (1¾ oz) Dutch (unsweetened) cocoa powder
20 g (¾ oz) baking powder
½ teaspoon bicarbonate of soda (baking soda)
125 g (4½ oz) Nutella, plus extra for topping
½ heaped teaspoon sea salt, plus extra
 for sprinkling

Preheat the oven to 170°C (340°F).

Combine the butter and sugars in a stand mixer fitted with the whisk attachment. Beat together on medium speed until well combined and lightly coloured. Do not overmix.

Add the eggs, one at a time, mixing well after each addition.

Add the remaining ingredients and whisk on low speed until well combined.

Line three baking trays with baking paper. Shape the cookie dough into 45 g (1½ oz) balls and place on the trays, spaced about 3 cm (1¼ in) apart to allow for spreading. Gently flatten them to about 1 cm (½ in) thick, then make a small dent in the centre of each cookie with your finger.

Place a generous 1½ teaspoons of Nutella in each of the dents. Sprinkle each cookie with a little sea salt.

Bake for 15 minutes, then transfer to a wire rack and leave to cool and crisp up before serving.

ABOUT THE AUTHOR

AMANDA RUBEN is the founder and owner of Miss Ruben, a New York–inspired deli and cafe in Ripponlea, in the heart of Melbourne's Jewish community.

The daughter of Jewish parents and a journalist by trade, Amanda grew up in the various kitchens of her entrepreneurial mother, Tamara, who ran a series of food businesses in Melbourne.

After switching careers, Amanda opened two food stores in partnership with her mum. Named after Amanda's two children, Cooper & Milla's offered amazing salads, cakes and simple food based around the best seasonal produce.

Miss Ruben has continued this theme, with a greater emphasis on catering and take-home food that subtly pays homage to the Jewish heritage of the area.

Amanda lives in Melbourne with her husband, Mark Gardy, and two children.

ACKNOWLEDGEMENTS

I can't say thank you enough to everyone involved in the making of this book.

When I ran Cooper & Milla's, customers asked me time and time again to do a cookbook, but I never imagined it would really happen one day. And if it wasn't for my tenacious, beautiful daughter, Milla, I might have let this one slip. I was so thankful to be approached by Hardie Grant with the idea of this book. But with Cooper's bar mitzvah just around the corner, followed six months later by Milla's bat mitzvah, a husband with a crazy work ethic, and a very new business to contend with, I decided there was no way I could fit this project in also. Milla told me otherwise and I'm so glad she did.

To my husband, Mark, and my kids, Cooper and Milla, thanks for making my life so full of fun, love and happiness. Mark, on top of managing your own extremely successful career, you step in whenever is needed to help me at home and at work, for which I am so very grateful. I hope we can travel together to all the places you dream of going to.

Milla, thanks for the beautiful cards you write me every birthday and mother's day – I'm so glad you've inherited your dad's special way with the written word. Thanks for all your help in the kitchen, both at home and as the best matzo ball roller at Miss Ruben, and your glass-half-full, can-do attitude to everything in life.

Cooper, thanks for your unbelievable wisdom, support and advice delivered in your usual matter-of-fact manner. Your mind works in a way mine never will. Thanks for teaching me how to use the point-of-sale system when I opened Miss Ruben and for all the kindness and understanding you've shown since I returned to work. I look forward to seeing where your business acumen takes you one day. And hope when you leave home you can make a mean chicken soup.

To my dad, Alex Ruben – in your quiet way you've always been there for Justin and I as a supporter and sounding board, and encouraged us to follow our ambitions. I have so much respect for the way you handled Mum's illness, and we're so glad to have you in our children's lives.

To my brother, Justin, sister-in-law, Giselle, and nieces, Sabine and Anouk, thanks for the advice on all that is cool via New York City. We miss having you in our day-to-day lives and cherish the times we are all together.

Of course my biggest acknowledgement is to my publisher, Hardie Grant, and its team for giving me this incredible opportunity. A very special thank you to the book's editor, Andrea O'Connor, for taking my pages and pages of at times indecipherable recipes and making them fit for *Feasting*, along with your tremendous support and encouragement at every point.

It was amazing to work with Deb Kaloper and Leesa O'Reilly, stylists whom I've admired for so long. And to Elisa Watson, thanks not only for your beautiful photos but also your generosity of spirit on the photo shoot.

This book would not have happened without my Miss Ruben team, in particular Bancha Boonchuen, Matthew Wihongi, Peta Santos and Jenny Quiroga. Not only have you helped to develop these recipes and to style and cook the food, but you also allowed me the time away from work to write. I'm so proud of the food we produce, and I owe so much of this to all of you.

To my gorgeous friends – who feel more like family – thanks for the walks, tuna patties and hippie treats. Thanks for supporting my business, and for being there with me always to commiserate and celebrate.

And to my customers, many of whom have followed me from Cooper & Milla's, and others who tell me stories about the functions my mum catered for them, thank you for coming and sharing my food journey.

INDEX

Published in 2018 by Hardie Grant Books,
an imprint of Hardie Grant Publishing

Hardie Grant Books (Melbourne)
Building 1, 658 Church Street
Richmond, Victoria 3121

Hardie Grant Books (London)
5th & 6th Floors
52–54 Southwark Street
London SE1 1UN

hardiegrantbooks.com

A Cataloguing-in-Publication entry is available from the catalogue
of the National Library of Australia at
www.nla.gov.au

Feasting: A new take on Jewish cooking
ISBN 978 1 74117 526 4

Publisher: Melissa Kayser
Managing Editor: Marg Bowman
Project Editor: Andrea O'Connor, Emily Hart
Editor: Susie Ashworth, Alison Proietto
Design Manager: Jessica Lowe
Designer: Kirby Armstrong
Photographer: Elisa Watson
Stylist: Deborah Kaloper, Matthew Wihongi, Leesa O'Rielly
Home Economist: Lindsay Harris
Typesetter: Megan Ellis
Indexer: Max McMaster
Production Manager: Todd Rechner
Production Coordinator: Tessa Spring

Colour reproduction by Splitting Image Colour Studio
Printed in China by 1010 Printing International Limited

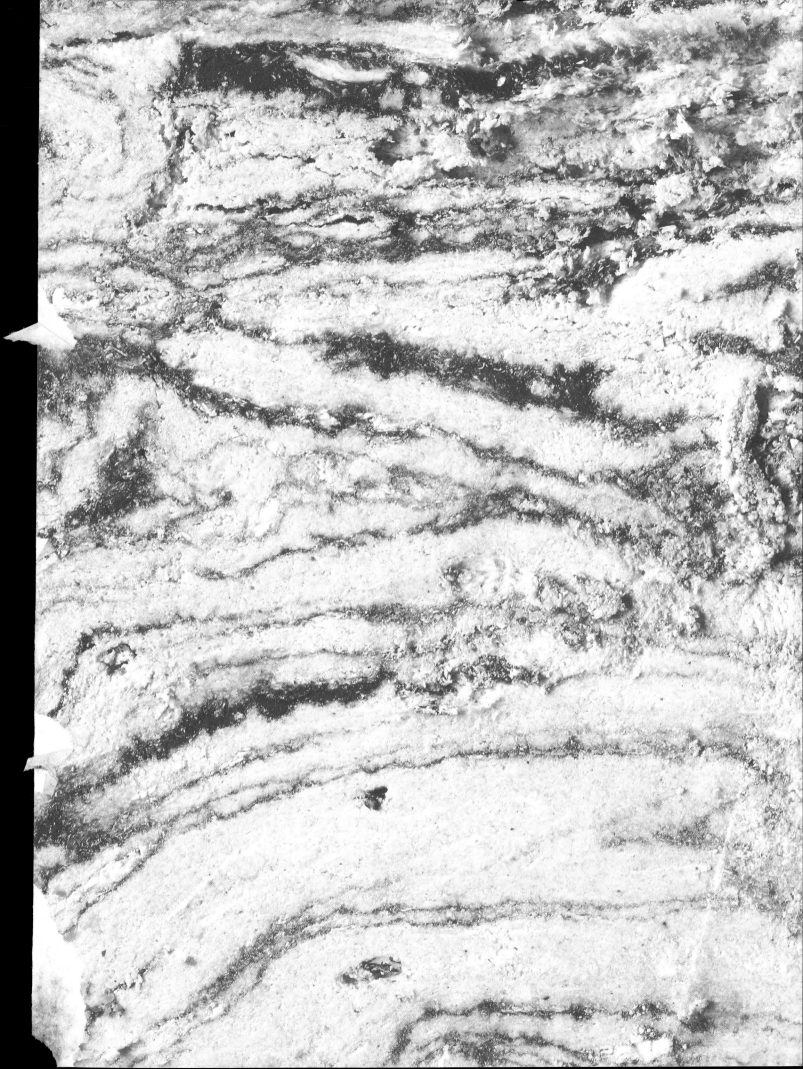

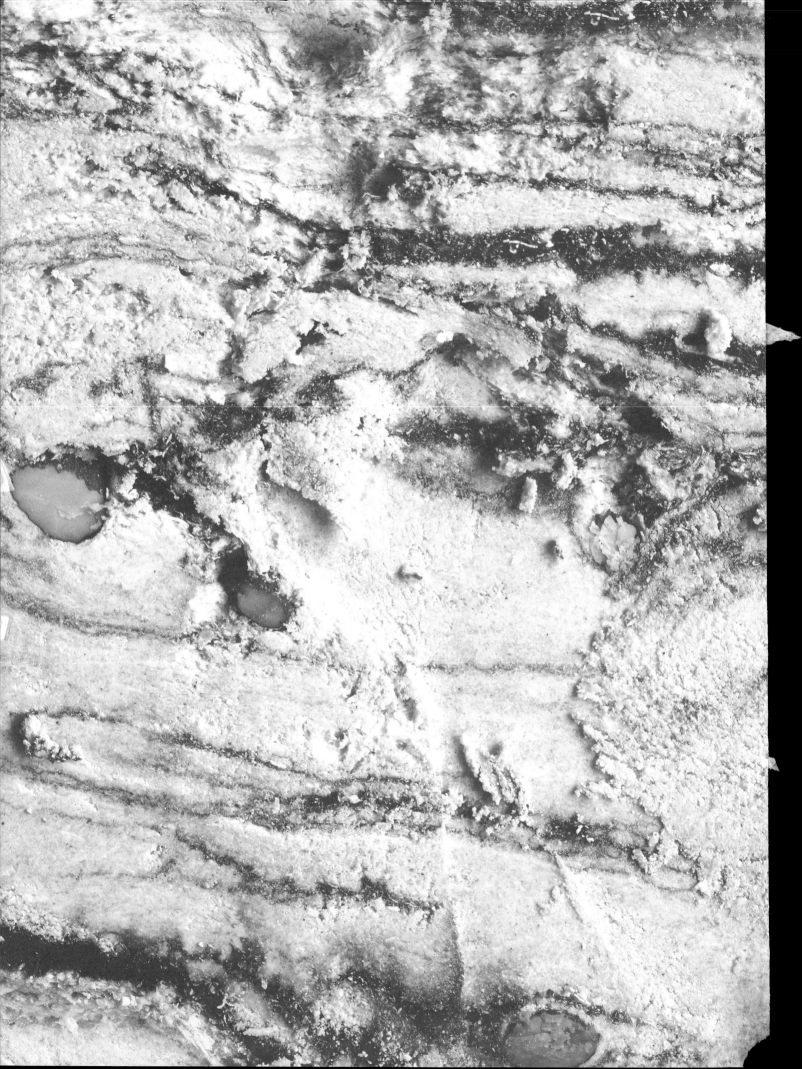